When Heaven Stands Open

When Heaven Stands Open

Liturgical Elements for Reformed Worship

~YEAR B~

Timothy Matthew Slemmons

CASCADE *Books* · Eugene, Oregon

WHEN HEAVEN STANDS OPEN
Liturgical Elements for Reformed Worship, Year B

Cascade Books
An Imprint of Wipf and Stock Publishers
199 W. 8ᵗʰ Ave., Suite 3
Eugene, OR 97401

www.wipfandstock.com

ISBN 13: 978-1-62032-001-3

Cataloguing-in-Publication Data

Slemmons, Timothy Matthew.

When heaven stands open : liturgical elements for reformed worship, year b / Timothy Matthew Slemmons.

xxvi + 230 pp. ; 23 cm. Includes bibliographical references and index(es).

ISBN 13: 978-1-62032-001-3

1. Common lectionary (1992)—Handbooks, manuals, etc. 2. Lectionaries—Handbooks, manuals, etc. 3. Reformed Church—Liturgy—Handbooks, manuals, etc. I. Title.

BX9427 .S57 2013

In memoriam does not quite apply,
as I have never met my eldest brother

—David Sheldon Slemmons—
(1947–1960)

so let us say this volume is offered to the glory of God
in joyful anticipation of our meeting in heaven
where God is all in all.

"O that you would tear open the heavens and come down,
so that the mountains would quake at your presence . . ."

Isaiah 64:1 (First Sunday of Advent)

Contents

Series Foreword | *xi*
Preface | *xix*
Acknowledgments | *xxiii*

Part I: The Christmas Cycle: *Advent—Christmas—Epiphany*

First Sunday of Advent | 3

Second Sunday of Advent | 6

Third Sunday of Advent | 9

Fourth Sunday of Advent | 12

Christmas, First Proper [ABC] *(Christmas Eve)* | 15

Christmas, Second Proper [ABC] *(Christmas Morning)* | 18

Christmas, Third Proper [ABC] *(Christmas Day)* | 21

First Sunday after Christmas | 24

Second Sunday after Christmas [ABC] | 27

Epiphany [ABC] | 30

First Sunday after Epiphany—Ordinary Time 1 *(Baptism of the Lord)* | 33

Second Sunday after Epiphany—Ordinary Time 2 | 36

Third Sunday after Epiphany—Ordinary Time 3 | 39

Fourth Sunday after Epiphany—Ordinary Time 4 | 42

Fifth Sunday after Epiphany—Ordinary Time 5 | 45

Sixth Sunday after Epiphany / Proper 1—Ordinary Time 6 | 48

Seventh Sunday after Epiphany / Proper 2—Ordinary Time 7 | 51

Eighth Sunday after Epiphany / Proper 3—Ordinary Time 8 | 54

Last Sunday after Epiphany *(Transfiguration Sunday)* | 57

Part II: The Paschal Cycle: *Lent—Easter—Pentecost*

Ash Wednesday [ABC] | 63

First Sunday in Lent | 66

Second Sunday in Lent | 69

Third Sunday in Lent | 72

Fourth Sunday in Lent | 75

Fifth Sunday in Lent | 78

Sixth Sunday in Lent *(Palm Sunday)* | 81

Seventh Sunday in Lent *(Passion Sunday)* | 84

Monday of Holy Week [ABC] | 87

Tuesday of Holy Week [ABC] | 90

Wednesday of Holy Week [ABC] | 93

Maundy Thursday [ABC] | 96

Good Friday [ABC] | 99

Easter *(The Resurrection of the Lord)* | 102

Easter Evening [ABC] | 105

Second Sunday of Easter | 108

Third Sunday of Easter | 111

Fourth Sunday of Easter | 114

Fifth Sunday of Easter | 117

Sixth Sunday of Easter | 120

Ascension of the Lord [ABC] | 123

Seventh Sunday of Easter | 126

Pentecost | 129

Part III: Ordinary Time (Propers 4–29): *Trinity—All Saints'—Christ the King*

Trinity Sunday | 135

Proper 4—Ordinary Time 9 / May 29–June 4 *(if after Trinity)* | 138

Proper 5—Ordinary Time 10 / June 5–11 *(if after Trinity)* | 141

Proper 6—Ordinary Time 11 / June 12–18 *(if after Trinity)* | 144

Proper 7—Ordinary Time 12 / June 19–25 *(if after Trinity)* | 147

Proper 8—Ordinary Time 13 / June 26–July 2 | 150

Proper 9—Ordinary Time 14 / July 3–9 | 153

Proper 10—Ordinary Time 15 / July 10–16 | 156

Proper 11—Ordinary Time 16 / July 17–23 | 159

Proper 12—Ordinary Time 17 / July 24–30 | 162

Proper 13—Ordinary Time 18 / July 31–August 6 | 165

Proper 14—Ordinary Time 19 / August 7–13 | 168

Proper 15—Ordinary Time 20 / August 14–20 | 171

Proper 16—Ordinary Time 21 / August 21–27 | 174

Proper 17—Ordinary Time 22 / August 28–September 3 | 177

Proper 18—Ordinary Time 23 / September 4–10 | 180

Proper 19—Ordinary Time 24 / September 11–17 | 183

Proper 20—Ordinary Time 25 / September 18–24 | 186

Proper 21—Ordinary Time 26 / September 25–October 1 | 189

Proper 22—Ordinary Time 27 / October 2–8 | 192

Proper 23—Ordinary Time 28 / October 9–15 | 195

Proper 24—Ordinary Time 29 / October 16–22 | 198

Proper 25—Ordinary Time 30 / October 23–29 | 201

Proper 26—Ordinary Time 31 / October 30–November 5 | 204

All Saints' Day / November 1 (or *First Sunday in November*) | 207

Proper 27—Ordinary Time 32 / November 6–12 | 210

Proper 28—Ordinary Time 33 / November 13–19 | 213

Proper 29—Ordinary Time 34 / November 20–26

(Christ the King or *Reign of Christ)* | 216

Index of Scripture Readings | 219

Series Foreword

THIS SERIES OF *LITURGICAL ELEMENTS FOR REFORMED WORSHIP* HAS developed over the course of more than fifteen years of ministry in Presbyterian contexts, primarily pastoral but also academic. Although this development has coincided with my own vocational (theological, homiletical, liturgical, and pastoral) formation and will therefore reflect a number of vocal variations (so to speak) that correspond to different stages of this formation, the primary concern that gave rise to this project in the first place has not diminished in the least, but has taken on an even deeper and more persistent sense of gravity and conviction. What began as a practical search for a greater variety of prayers of confession and assurances than I found in the *Book of Common Worship* (1993)— and more specifically, for prayers that reflected more directly how the Church should confess in response to specific texts found in the *Revised Common Lectionary* (1992) from week to week—has become an overriding concern that informs both my work in advocating an expansion of the lectionary, as well as my labors in the area of Reformed homiletics and worship, namely, that ongoing and continual repentance from sin in all its forms is essential, not accidental, to the Christian life, to the Reformed tradition of worship, and to the vitality and viability of the Church.

Reared as so many other pastors and seminary students have been on the textbooks of the late liturgical scholar James F. White, an ecumenically minded Methodist who served on the faculty at Notre Dame, I too quickly and uncritically adopted White's dim characterization of Reformed worship that he repeatedly describes (at least in the hands of the Swiss Reformers and their Calvinist and Puritan descendants) as "heavily penitential." This negative caricature is reinforced so often by White[1] and in the literature developed in his wake that his more posi-

---

1. James F. White, *Introduction to Christian Worship,* 3rd ed. (Nashville: Abingdon, 2000) 124, 160, 161, 189, 254, 256, et al., and *A Brief History of Christian Worship*

tive assessment of the joy with which the same tradition sang the Psalms seems jarringly inconsistent, that is, as though the connection between repentance and the joyful freedom to be discovered therein is entirely incongruous. Equally symptomatic of White's failure to appreciate the Reformed tradition is his suggestion that Calvin simply followed the Fourth Lateran Council in requiring confession before communion, as though the premier theologian of the sixteenth century applied the scriptural regulative principle to every question but this one.

White was not alone in his superficial (i.e., dour) understanding of the Reformed tradition, of course, but his conviction that "the study of Christian worship is the best way to learn ecumenism" has been influential and probably explains why many Reformed liturgical scholars today seem more eager to shun whatever may be described as "heavily penitential" than to lay claim to the true character of the Reformed tradition as *essentially* penitential, and not merely in a manner that belongs to the medieval period, from which, the ecumenist White suggests, the Reformers were not sufficiently critical to separate themselves. On the contrary, the point that should appear obvious to those who apply the principle of canonical comprehensiveness[2] in their study of Scripture and the regulative principle to their study of the Reformation is that the Reformers, in their own exegetical labors, discerned the summons to repentance resounding throughout the canon and (despite important differences in grammatical moods) on both sides of the crucifixion, resurrection, and ascension of Jesus, and they felt sufficiently convinced and convicted by it that they sought to give it a central and essential, not an auxiliary role, in their liturgical reforms. As I have said elsewhere, this essential role of repentance is signaled at least symbolically, and perhaps definitively, in the fact that the first of Luther's ninety-five theses (1517), the initial downbeat of the Reformation itself, declares that the Christian life is one of ongoing repentance. Meanwhile, the liturgical renewal movement, driven in part by the desire to avoid medieval stereotypes, has succeeded in depriving the Reformed worship tradition of one of its greatest, most distinctive, and powerful gifts: the disciplines of self-examination and robust confession that are the hallmark of true repentance and deep "reform." The services of preparation and self-examination (that last appeared in the

---

(Nashville: Abingdon, 1993) 76, 105, et al.

2. See Timothy Matthew Slemmons, *Year D: A Quadrennial Supplement to the Revised Common Lectionary* (Eugene, OR: Cascade, 2012).

1946 edition of the *Book of Common Worship*) have given way before the drive toward more frequent communion, and one can only wonder at what point, if ever, the trend toward less preparation and more "celebration" will bring to mind the long forgotten and much abused dialectic of the holy and the common.

It is from this point of deep conviction that this series of liturgical resources is sent forth, not because every element will necessarily do justice to the sense in which perpetual repentance is the most frequently overlooked and distinctive "essential tenet" of the Reformed tradition (and because the most distinctive, therefore the most essential, so to speak), but for the simple fact that repentance, self-examination, confession, and the good news of forgiveness deserve far better than to be reduced to the formulaic. It may well be that those who worship in the Reformed tradition, at least those who are unembarrassed by the essentially penitential—and undeniably joyful—character of the tradition, are best positioned to lay claim to that truth and offer it to the broader Church. On the other hand, anyone who would persist in such embarrassment, I would suggest, is not paying sufficient attention—to Scripture, to the state of the Church, to the state of the world, or the state of their own souls.

This is not to say that these elements come from on high, by any stretch, except insofar as they are a response to, and sometimes a direct voicing of, Scripture. Rather, these prayers come from the pen of one who needs to pray them. They were in no instance designed to be prescriptive, but are the best response this pastor has been able to muster as one who finds himself staring down the business end of the sword of the Word (Eph 6:17; Heb 4:12; Rev 2:12; 19:15, 21). But what a startling thing it was the first time I heard a congregation praying in unison a Prayer of Confession I had written and printed in the bulletin! Having shifted my focus entirely from the task of getting the bulletin together on Thursday afternoon to entering into worship itself on Sunday morning, I was halfway through the prayer myself before I realized: "These words sound familiar." Then it dawned on me: "Oh, yes. I wrote them."

There was nothing especially gratifying about this experience, for I have never harbored any great aspiration to put words in other people's mouths. But from that moment the prospect of writing prayers that the people of God themselves would speak in worship became a particularly sobering and serious responsibility. For, in fact, there is an inescapable sense in which "finding words for worship"[3] does in effect put words in the mouths of those in attendance: individuals of innumerable dispositions, including some who may well resist assenting (saying "Amen") to them, and churches (local, denominational, and global) whose spiritual and moral conditions need to be truthfully and honestly confessed in the presence of "God and everybody." It is no exaggeration whatsoever, but theologically and anthropologically accurate, to say that the Prayer of Confession can, by its very nature as an expression and an act of repentance, "make one's flesh crawl," for repentance is a gift from God (Acts 5:31; 11:18), but "the mind that is set on the flesh is hostile to God; it does not submit to God's law—indeed it cannot . . ." (Rom 8:6–7). Prayers of Confession then must walk a fine line, balancing "brutal" honesty with tender mercy; they must break the horse, not make it bolt.

The responsibility for liturgy is incalculably heightened when one considers that such prompting of the people is no mere stage direction; yet, per Kierkegaard's *contra*-theatrical analogy, the minister or preacher *is* a prompter whose labor is done with the expectation that the people will in fact direct the prompted words *to God*. And as if *this* were not enough, the pastor and liturgist must remember that the liturgy at points entails speaking *for* God to the people—as in the Declaration of Forgiveness, which bears the liberating function of Gospel every bit as much as does the preaching of the Word. *God* calls the people to worship. *The risen Jesus Christ* heralds the good news of forgiveness. Worship is less a work of the people (who are but the minor partners in the conversation) and more a work of *the Holy Spirit*. Yet *the Holy Trinity* condescends to enlist human agents in doing all of this work (externally speaking), much of it through the pastor as liturgist. Sobering thoughts indeed.

But such a responsibility cannot be fulfilled by a formulaic approach. The routinization of worship is deadly, even if it results from the most faithful allegiance to orthodoxy. As one pastoral colleague put the problem when I entered into this project some fifteen years ago, "So how many ways can you say, 'You are forgiven!'?" That is certainly one way of posing the question. How should one answer? To begin with: more than three.[4] On the one hand, the words of Scripture themselves are the sole written authority and norm for all elements of worship, including the Declaration

3. See Ruth Duck, *Finding Words for Worship: A Guide for Leaders* (Louisville: Westminster John Knox, 1995).

4. *Book of Common Worship* (Louisville: Westminster John Knox, 1993) 56–57.

of Forgiveness. On the other hand, the same Spirit who speaks through the Scriptures resists distillation of the singular gospel to a single formula, but inspires ongoing interpretation, reiteration, amplification, and elaboration as required by a wide variety of human conditions; for sin, depravity, guilt, pride, and all manner of things that exalt themselves in opposition to the Word (2 Cor 10:4) may succeed against incantation, but they will not succeed against the Church at worship recapitulating the *missio Dei* in fresh, biblically faithful ways. The Word of the LORD will not return empty (Isa 55), and the gates of hell will not prevail against the Church (Matt 16) *at worship*. As J.-J. von Allmen observed (specifically with reference to 1 Cor 11–14), the term *ecclesia* first and foremost applies to the liturgical assembly; it is not primarily a sociological term.[5] This insight, clear as it is in Scripture, has yet to sink in to the mind of the mainline churches, which seem entirely bent on sociological reform. But if von Allmen was right, and I think he was, then I would contend that the diversity of the Church need not be forced to satisfy our sociological presuppositions, whether liberal or conservative, but allowed to arise in and emerge from worship itself as the Church encounters the risen Christ and the Holy Spirit speaking through the Scriptures.

Further, if we follow this understanding of an essentially liturgical ecclesiology, and an essentially repentant orientation to the Christian life, through to their logical conclusion and point of convergence, we must finally recognize the fact that, in the temporal sphere (and whether we like it or not), Christian worship cannot be fully grasped apart from the theater of spiritual warfare by which it is surrounded and from which it is protected and held *in God* as a sanctuary—a holy "safe" zone, so to speak—an assembly around font, pulpit, and table, with the whole creation (Rom 8:19), even a host of impotent enemies (Ps 23:5), looking on.

"Safe," of course, is a relative term and begs definition in relation to its distinct referents. I would not be so naïve in this day and age to suggest that physical harm cannot come to God's people in worship, but I shall say with the psalmist, "I trust in God; I am not afraid; what can flesh do to me?" (Ps 56:4) Neither would I suggest that the holy presence of God is unambiguously "safe," so as to lose sight of the "fear of the LORD" that is due him (Ps 90:11). Nevertheless, when worship is framed in this way, the Church stands to gain a much clearer sense of what is at stake, and to

---

5. J.-J. von Allmen, *Worship: Its Theology and Practice* (New York: Oxford University Press, 1965) 43.

see people of every spiritual condition avail themselves of the healing and salvific presence of the Lord, even as worship itself serves (esthetically) as creation's libretto in the theatre of God's glory, the theatre in which "the battle is the LORD's" and the Church's vocation is to remember and give thanks for victories past and promised. As von Allmen held:

> in its liturgy the Church acts on behalf of the world, which is to-tally incapable of adoring and glorifying the true God, and . . . the Church [at worship] represents the world before God and protects it.[6]

In other words, the Church, as a royal priesthood in Christ, has an inter-cessory role to play whereby its worship, as it were, actually "protects" the world. That alone should be both good news to the whole Church and good news to the world! Hence, liturgy is really not "common worship" in any sense. On the contrary, liturgy is the divine and priestly service of the body of Christ, the service of worship performed by the Church—as it is empowered, guided, and inspired by the Holy Spirit—for God and in response to God's gracious self-revelation in the Servant Lord Jesus Christ. True liturgy unfolds under the headship, under the most excellent ministry (liturgy), and in the name of Jesus Christ, the Son of God, in whom all believers together are to serve in a united yet diversely gifted priesthood, to the eternal glory of God—and (temporarily) on behalf of a liturgically incompetent and often hostile world.

These convictions, as mentioned above, have come very slowly.[7] While I hope in future to be able to articulate these concerns and convic-tions more clearly and thoroughly (and defend them, if necessary), for now I must admit the evidence of this unlovely developmental plodding may be all too obvious in the liturgical elements provided here and in the three companion volumes that are planned. For this project has developed contemporaneously with my own continuing theological education and vocation, and in the weekly attempt to prepare faithful worship amidst the numerous competing demands of life and ministry; thus, all stages of this development will be represented here. This will account for the varying degrees of tone: from solemnity to exuberance, from the poetic to the prosaic, from an initial concern for avoiding overuse of masculine

6. Ibid., 16.

7. As I say frequently and with no irony intended, I loosely translate the Latin on my own PhD (*philosophiae doctor*) degree to read, "slow learner."

metaphors for God to a more intentional use of the biblical names of God, including LORD and Lord, etc., and a desire to avoid the far greater sin of effectively depersonalizing God by the avoidance of personal pronouns. (Where the use of LORD is concerned, my intention has been to retain this reference to the tetragrammaton, YHWH, as it is rendered in most translations of the Old Testament, and thereby direct the reader's attention to the holy name as it is used in the texts that inspired the element in question; likewise, the use of Lord is meant to reflect usage in the New Testament, which most often occurs in reference to Jesus.) In light of this peculiarly developmental quality, then, the reader may find it more helpful to approach these volumes as more of an indicative historical record, as useful artifacts, than as prescriptive in any heavy-handed or "heavily penitential" sense. They are perhaps a tidy presentation of the otherwise untidy relics of many services, a peek into one pastor's file drawers stuffed with bulletins and prayers prepared for congregations perhaps very different from the reader's own. Many, if not most, of these elements, if they are to be of service to the ongoing life of the Church at worship, will invite adaptation, in which case I simply ask that those who thus adapt them will acknowledge doing so, yet remember with kindness and favor the congregations, both the saints and their pastor, whence and among whom—by the grace of the Word and the Spirit—they first arose.

Timothy Matthew Slemmons
University of Dubuque Theological Seminary
The Feast of Epiphany, A.D. 2012

Preface

THERE ARE MANY SCRIPTURE PASSAGES THAT TESTIFY TO VISIONS OF THE kingdom behind the veil, moments when the curtain has been decisively rent and the ineffable revealed. Not all of these passages find their way into the *Revised Common Lectionary*. Notably, the following passages are excluded.

> In the thirtieth year, in the fourth month, on the fifth day of the month, as I was among the exiles by the river Chebar, the heavens were opened, and I saw visions of God. (Ezek 1:1)

> He saw the heaven opened and something like a large sheet coming down, being lowered to the ground by its four corners. (Acts 10:11)

> After this I looked, and there in heaven a door stood open! And the first voice, which I had heard speaking to me like a trumpet, said, "Come up here, and I will show you what must take place after this." (Rev 4:1)

> Then God's temple in heaven was opened, and the ark of his covenant was seen within his temple; and there were flashes of lightning, rumblings, peals of thunder, an earthquake, and heavy hail. (Rev 11:19)

> Then I saw heaven opened, and there was a white horse! Its rider is called Faithful and True, and in righteousness he judges and makes war. (Rev 19:11)

While years A, B, and C each contain their narrowly selected apocalyptic allusions to heaven's openings, particularly in Advent, nevertheless Year B contains some of the most explicit references, which appear at key points of the calendar. The year assigned to Mark's Gospel (with assistance from John) begins with this image from Isaiah, unequivocally the evangelist's favorite prophet, on the First Sunday of Advent.

> O that you would tear open the heavens and come down,
>   so that the mountains would quake at your presence . . . . (Isa 64:1)

Mark's account of the baptism of Jesus, read on the First Sunday after Epiphany, contains the same image, as does the calling of the first disciples in John, appearing the following week.

> And just as he was coming up out of the water, he saw the heavens torn apart and the Spirit descending like a dove on him. (Mark 1:10; Baptism of the Lord and the First Sunday in Lent)

> Jesus answered, "Do you believe because I told you that I saw you under the fig tree? You will see greater things than these." And he said to [Nathanael], "Very truly, I tell you, you will see heaven opened and the angels of God ascending and descending upon the Son of Man." (John 1:50–51; Second Sunday after Epiphany)

At the other end of Jesus' earthly ministry, the Passion Sunday narrative reaches its climax with this mysterious but wonderfully omniscient pronouncement:

> Then Jesus gave a loud cry and breathed his last. And the curtain of the temple was torn in two, from top to bottom. (Mark 15:37–38; Passion Sunday)

The image of heaven opening, neither circumscribed by the lectionary nor exclusive to Year B, nevertheless figures most prominently here, especially when compared to a singular but relatively inconspicuous occurrence in Year A, where the Acts sequence replaces the Old Testament reading in the weeks following Easter. The revelation occurs in Luke's account of the stoning of Stephen, itself a reminder of the Passion.

> "Look," [Stephen] said, "I see the heavens opened and the Son of Man standing at the right hand of God!" (Acts 7:56)

Why isolate this one image from the whole liturgical year? What is the worship of God, the praise of the risen Christ, the invocation of the Holy Spirit without heaven opening? "For where two or three are gathered in my name, I am there among them" (Matt 18:20). What is Reformed worship without the eschatological understanding that we are uplifted by the Holy Spirit into the presence of the ascended Christ?

The prayers and elements presented here were initially assembled as part of my ministerial duties in a small congregation, the Central

Presbyterian Church in Tarentum, Pennsylvania, and repeatedly edited and reworked in the years since my service there concluded. The result will not win any awards for eliminating, or even balancing, all gender-specific references to God, but neither has it aspired to do so. It does not perpetuate masculine references to humanity, save indirectly, where Christ Jesus is mentioned as the Son of Man, a title far too important to lose for the sake of lesser aims.

My hope for the four volumes in this series of liturgical elements is that they might (1) simply glorify the triune God and build up both the individual worshipper and the Church in faith, and (2) serve as occasion for the convergence of the doxological Spirit and the scriptural revelation of the Word—for worship "in spirit and in truth"—with both vitality and integrity, that genuine worship of the Holy God may prove its esthetic validity in faith. Despite the need for judicious application, adaptation, refinement and ongoing revision of the elements, may this resource and its companion volumes, like the synoptic authors and like the three painters in Rilke's wondrous story, "go on painting him till they die themselves."

> God does not appear every day, nor yet to everybody. And of course each of the three thought God was standing to *him alone*. . . . And every time God wants to go back into the sky again, Saint Luke begs him to stay out a while longer, until the three painters have finished their pictures.[8]

Luke shall have his say in Year C. Meanwhile, as heaven stands open, the holy, eternal, triune God awaits those who come to praise, to petition, to preach, and if the Reformed pastor may do so without risk of idolatry, to paint!

---

8. Rainer Maria Rilke, "A Society Sprung of Urgent Need," in *Stories of God*, translated by M. D. Herter Norton (New York: Norton, 1963) 97–107, quotation on 106.

Acknowledgments

ANY VOLUME OF LITURGICAL ELEMENTS FOR CHRISTIAN WORSHIP IN THE Reformed tradition must necessarily begin and end and be permeated throughout with thanksgiving and praise to the triune God. *Soli Deo Gloria!* But while the Trinity has also determined, by virtue of the grace of God's revelation, incarnation, mission, and covenantal nature, to involve and enlist many saints in the ongoing ministry of the Word and the Spirit, and while there are innumerable agents of God's grace for whom I do give thanks at this juncture, I will confine myself to mentioning those whose roles loom largest in my admittedly porous memory.

First of all, and most instrumentally, I give thanks for the two congregations I have been blessed to serve as pastor and interim pastor, respectively, for it is these congregations that gave voice and lent their communal "Amen" to these various elements, or something close to them: Central Presbyterian Church, Tarentum, Pennsylvania (1995–2000), and First Presbyterian Church, Titusville, New Jersey (2004–2008).

The gracious pedagogical comments of the late Dr. Lucy Rose of Columbia Seminary continue to be instructive each time I teach worship. The prayers of the Reverend Roy Henderson at Lansdowne Parish Church, Glasgow, UK, a fine wordsmith, fed me for a year's worth of Sundays abroad, while the leaders of the Late Late Service, also in Glasgow, likewise challenged me by example to think through the words used in worship with painstaking care (1992–93). Dr. Fred Anderson's labors at Madison Avenue Presbyterian Church and his enormous contribution to the worship of the Presbyterian Church (USA) are well documented, and I am grateful for the encouragement he has offered in our few brief but memorable exchanges.

The shape of Lavon Bayler's worship resources—*Taught By Love; Led By Love;* and *Gathered By Love* (United Church Press)—which I ran across in 1996 and have used on occasion, inspired the notion that

I might be able to build a similar resource over time, but in a more Reformed voice and vein.

Dr. Richard Young, now at Orchard Park Presbyterian Church in the Buffalo, New York area, offered encouragement early on, and he was a rare and delightful conversation partner when we were both serving in western Pennsylvania.

My professors at Princeton Seminary—specifically, Dr. James F. Kay (now Dean), Dr. Sally Brown, and visiting lecturer Dr. Hughes Oliphant Old (now Dean of Erskine Seminary's Institute for Reformed Worship)—prompted more critical (and self-critical) thinking about liturgical concerns, and I am grateful for their instruction in seminars, in their pedagogy, and in their scholarship.

I am also grateful to the First Presbyterian Church, Topeka, Kansas, which has served as my "safe home" sanctuary for going on fifty years. I am especially grateful to the long line of ministers, musicians, and other saints who have served that congregation over the years and maintained a highly esthetic doxology; the Reverend C. Michael Kuner, who once served the church as both Associate Pastor and later as Interim Head of Staff, is my brother-in-law and has served as a mentor for many years; Mike's wife and my sister, Jennifer Kuner, has often filled the sanctuary with her exquisite solo (and choral) contributions, carrying on the contralto reverberations our mother first put in motion beginning in the 1940s. Ashley Smith, of Cleveland, Ohio, a Presbyterian elder who works with the Cleveland Youth Orchestra; Karen Smith of Oakmont, Pennsylvania, a frequent soprano soloist; and her mother (and Ashley's grandmother), the late Betty Hicks, a lifelong organist, joined in or initiated numerous discussions of worship through the years, and one is ever mindful of key considerations in light thereof. Of course, I am most grateful that the Lord saw fit to bring me into the world through, and place me in the care of, two of the most loving and gracious parents a child could ever hope for: my mother, Dorothy Herrick Slemmons, and my late father, Robert Sheldon Slemmons. I continually give thanks, and I do so again now, that my parents raised me in the Church: Sunday school, worship, youth choir, bell choir, youth groups, etc., every week whenever each was in session.

Finally, I give thanks for Victoria, for whom worship is, not just theory but in reality, the most joyous daily activity. I bless the Lord for her ministry in prayer, in song, and at the harp, for the sweetness of her voice and her spirit, and for the lovely sounds of her inspired psalm settings, to say nothing of all the other dimensions of the life of Christian marriage and friendship that we share in Christ. Nevertheless, *Come, Lord Jesus!*

PART I

The Christmas Cycle
Advent—Christmas—Epiphany

First Sunday of Advent

Isaiah 64:1–9

Psalm 80:1–7, 17–19

1 Corinthians 1:3–9

Mark 13:24–37

In Preparation for Worship

We look to you in our eager longing.
Come to us, Immanuel.
We await your revealing,
your enthronement in our hearts to reign over us,
your return to this world to restore creation.
Amen. Come, Lord Jesus!

Call to Worship

God is faithful! Come together and wait for the advent of the Lord.
We lack nothing for the vigil. We keep watch and wait.
Stay awake! For you do not know when the Lord will return.
With signs in the heavens,
with power and glory, Christ will come.
Take heart! By the grace of God you have been blessed.
We will endure to the end, that we may be found blameless
when Jesus Christ comes again.

Opening Prayer

Eternal God, who comes to us in different forms and at different times, we
await your coming again: Let the heavens be opened! Let every creature

on earth behold your grandeur and your glory! We anticipate your arrival with worship in our hearts, with eager, expectant eyes, and with lives ready to be changed by your holy presence among us.

CALL TO CONFESSION

Scripture tells us that we all have become unclean and our sin, like the wind, uproots us. Sin happens when we fail to call upon the name of the LORD, when we fail to reach for God and take hold. Let us seek the LORD's face, confess our sin, and ask for deliverance.

PRAYER OF CONFESSION

O God, you are the great artisan, shaping us like clay pots, fulfilling your purpose in us. Yet we resist your will, refusing to take the shape which you intend for us. We are stubborn when we should surrender to your design, and we are passive when we should take righteous action. Forgive our disobedience, and strengthen us in faith. Refresh us for the task of waiting on you and for you.

WORDS OF ASSURANCE

Scripture assures us that we are called by none other than God to share in the life of Jesus Christ our Lord, and, we are told, God keeps faith. To the extent that we take seriously God's will for us to live in Christ, and faithfully seek to do so, surely we need not sin again. Therefore, live into Christ in faith, knowing that your sins are absolved through Christ, by Christ, and in Christ.

PRESENTATION OF TITHES AND OFFERINGS

The time has come to place our gifts at the LORD's disposal. At the end, Christ will gather in all of the chosen ones. For now, let us offer up, for God's ingathering, our hearts and our minds, along with our gifts, trusting that the LORD will make use of the fruit of our life together for the advancement of Christ's kingdom, which will soon come in glory.

PRAYER OF DEDICATION

God of faith, Christ of glory, Spirit of growth, there is so much work to be done. None of it will happen without you: you to inspire the vision, you to light the way, you to catch desire on fire in our hearts. May these gifts become yours again, that you would lay a foundation of hope with them, for the redemption of the world through the coming of your kingdom.

RESPONSIVE BLESSING

We live in a time of waiting.
> **We are as servants who wait upon God, the master.**

We are as parents awaiting the coming of
the glorious and holy Christ child.
> **We are disciples,**
> **awaiting the coming of the promised Spirit.**

Go. Your waiting will not be in vain.
> **Amen! Come, Lord Jesus!**

Second Sunday of Advent

Isaiah 40:1–11
Psalm 85:1–2, 8–13
2 Peter 3:8–15a
Mark 1:1–8

In Preparation for Worship

We wait for you, little knowing that you wait for us to reach out.
We call to you, heedless of your voice in our ears.
We approach you, making no forward progress, but turning around,
we discover you have been with us all along.

Call to Worship

The prophets of old prepared the righteous way,
and called the people of God to return to the Lord.
> **So shall we return to the kingdom**
> **where Christ, by the law of mercy, reigns.**
Let the heavens open, and the Spirit of God come down.
The reward of God is for those who seek the kingdom.
> **So shall we be baptized with water and the Holy Spirit,**
> **into the forgiveness of sins, into the ways of faith.**
Even as we wait for the Lord,
God is patiently waiting for us.
> **So shall we learn to walk in God's ways,**
> **for in God's patience is our salvation.**

OPENING PRAYER

God of our salvation, you speak peace and act patiently toward those who trust in you. Therefore, we turn our hearts to you in faith. Let the light of your glory dwell among us. Let peace and prosperity come to us as you restore us to your salvation.

CALL TO CONFESSION

The first baptism by John in the river Jordan is described in Mark as a baptism of repentance into forgiveness of sins, and those John baptized were baptized confessing their sins. Let us also repent of sin, beginning with confession.

PRAYER OF CONFESSION

O God and Father of our Lord Jesus Christ, we confess that we have not prepared a straight path for you. Our lives are full of hills and valleys, detours into sin, errant and aimless wanderings. Our mouths are treacherous. Our hearts are fickle. Forgive us for our sins, O God, and forget our former ways. By the grace of your Son and the power of the Holy Spirit, cleanse us anew and give us faithful hearts, ready for humble service in your kingdom.

DECLARATION OF FORGIVENESS

Scripture assures us that God's will is for none to be lost, and that all should come to repentance. Indeed, we are told to regard God's patience with us as our salvation. Patience is a willing endurance, and in Jesus Christ we have seen all that God is willing to suffer that we might be saved. Friends, know that forgiveness is found in Jesus Christ. Christ is alive! Christ is coming! Therefore, be at peace.

PRESENTATION OF TITHES AND OFFERINGS

The psalmist sings of justice peering down from heaven, and faithfulness straining towards the sky; of God raining down prosperity from heaven, and the land showing forth a harvest. Grace becomes a two-way street. God gives us prosperity and justice, but we must remember our part in the relationship, which is to be faithful and fruitful with all that we have. Let us offer our gifts to God in good faith.

PRAYER OF DEDICATION

God who was, and is, and is to come, we remember how you have provided for us. For you have brought us to this time and place, our future is in your capable, caring, and gracious hands, and you are trustworthy in all things. So take these gifts as your own, and work your good will with them, for the honor and glory of your Son and our Savior, Jesus Christ.

RESPONSIVE BLESSING

The LORD is coming! Prepare the way!
> **We wait with faith for Christ's coming in glory.**

The LORD is not slow. Christ is coming quickly!
> **We go forth to make straight paths for our God.**

The LORD is gracious and good, slow to anger and abounding in mercy.
> **Truly God's patience is our salvation. Amen. Come, Lord Jesus!**

Third Sunday of Advent

Isaiah 61:1–4, 8–11
Psalm 126 OR Luke 1:47–55
1 Thessalonians 5:16–24
John 1:6–8, 19–28

IN PREPARATION FOR WORSHIP
Sanctify us, O God.
Make us whole and holy,
in spirit, soul, and body.
We hold fast to you, forsaking former ways,
claiming our covenant with you and in you.

CALL TO WORSHIP
May the Spirit of the LORD be with us.
The Light of God is our guide through life.
Let us follow that light,
the beacon leading to the miracle birth.
May the Spirit of Love burn within us.
Do not quench its fire!
Let us hold to what is good,
trusting in the prophecies of old.
Come to Bethlehem and see!
The Word of the LORD is coming to life!
We seek the Light of Christ.
The God of peace is with us!

Opening Prayer

Light of the world, we have come to witness your glory, that we might bear witness to the world that we have seen you and known you. Come and make yourself known to us, and to the world through us, in Jesus' name.

Call to Confession

John the Baptist confessed that he was not worthy to untie the thong of Jesus' sandals! Then where do we stand? Surely also among the unworthy! As John confessed who he was: not the Christ, not Elijah, not the Prophet; let us confess who we are: sinners in need of grace.

Prayer of Confession

God of justice and peace, you come to proclaim release to captives, yet we remain imprisoned by so much sin and self-doubt. We remain within the walls of our dark dungeons, heedless of the door hanging off its hinges. We are free, yet deluded by sin into remaining its slaves, even though its power is a lie. Forgive us, and light our way out of this darkness. Lead us out into the bright night sky, and show us your holy light, that we may be led to the Christ.

Declaration of Forgiveness

Christ has come to bring gladness to replace our sorrow, a new garland instead of ashes. Surely God blesses us despite our sin, proclaiming a Jubilee, a year of the LORD's favor, so that the world might learn a new definition of justice: God's justice, which is rooted in the rich earth of forgiveness, producing shoots of praise and good will!

Presentation of Tithes and Offerings

The psalmist rejoices that God has done great things for us. The apostle tells us to give thanks in everything. Let us now do our very best for God, showing our gratitude with our gifts.

Prayer of Dedication

God of peace, you are our model of faithfulness. We commend these gifts to your use, as our act of faith in you. Sanctify them, and sanctify us, that-eternal joy and goodness might mark those who uplift your holy name; that such joy might draw others toward your wonderful light; that we might be found blameless in spirit, soul, and body, at your coming in glory.

THE BLESSING

As the Baptist bore witness to the Light, go into the world remembering your baptism, for you too have been bathed in the Light. Tell the world of the Light you have seen, and bathe it in the light of Christ's redeeming love.

Fourth Sunday of Advent

2 Samuel 7:1–11, 16

Luke 1:47–55 OR Psalm 89:1–4, 19–26

Romans 16:25–27

Luke 1:26–38

IN PREPARATION FOR WORSHIP

God of creation, who fills the empty with good things:
I come to you empty.
God of holiness, who invests the barren with life:
I come to you barren.
God of the annunciation, who blesses the trusting with promises fulfilled:
I receive you in trust.
Let my soul magnify you!

CALL TO WORSHIP

The LORD of Hosts journeys with us.
God shall assign a place for us.
> **The LORD has no need of cedar,**
> **no house built by human hands.**
God has spoken through shepherds: through David
and those who worshipped the holy child.
> **God's chosen servant will rule as long as the heavens endure.**
The promises of God can never fail!
God's mercy is sure from generation to generation.
> **This child is the Son of the Most High!**
> **Born of a woman! The Son of God!**

OPENING PRAYER

Almighty God, who raises up the humble and lowly, who brings down the arrogant and insolent, we magnify you, as Mary did in song, as Joseph did in trust, that your living word of love might come to fruition and full maturity in us, for your glory. We ask this in the name of your Son, Jesus Christ.

CALL TO CONFESSION

God's justice is not predominantly that everyone be compensated for everything they have done, good or bad, but that everyone comes to know he or she is loved by God. The kingdom of God is founded on righteousness which is faithfulness, on justice which is love. Let us confess our sins, trusting in our loving God.

PRAYER OF CONFESSION

God of humble beginnings, we confess we have failed to trust you to lift us out of our lowly state. We have been guided by a spirit of pride and one-upmanship, exalting ourselves at the expense of your children. Forgive us for our many sins and restore us to an attitude of humility, gratitude, and loving faith, that we may be found without fault when we meet the Christ, in whose name we pray.

DECLARATION OF FORGIVENESS

God's promises are sure. The love of God never ends. The Word of God has been born into the midst of a sinful world, so as to forgive, redeem, and restore God's creatures to a right relationship with the LORD. Those who call upon the LORD shall find shelter, the safety of a loving Father, against whom no enemy, not even sin or death, can prevail. Believe the gospel. In Jesus Christ, we are forgiven.

PRESENTATIONS OF TITHES AND OFFERINGS

Mary and Elizabeth gave of their own flesh and blood to nurture God's holy servants. Joseph entrusted his fiancé to the LORD, putting his own rights aside. Ultimately, all parents surrender control over their dear children to the hope of the destiny to which God calls them. What gifts shall we surrender to the LORD?

PRAYER OF DEDICATION

Holy God, we surrender these possessions to you, forsaking our owner-ship of them, acknowledging your sovereignty over all that we own, all that we have brought into the world, all that we have taken from it, and, ultimately, all that we are. Consecrate these your gifts to us, that as we return them to you, your kingdom might be established on earth, and your holy name magnified.

A RESPONSIVE BLESSING

The one who called God 'Father' is come: Christ, the firstborn of all creation!

To the only wise God, through Jesus Christ, be glory forever!
God's reign is just and founded on love. There is no end to God's mercy!

To the only wise God, through Jesus Christ, be glory forever!
Fear not, for the LORD is exceedingly gracious.
May God's will be done in you.

To the only wise God, through Jesus Christ, be glory forever!

Christmas, First Proper (ABC)
Christmas Eve

Isaiah 9:2–7

Psalm 96

Titus 2:11–14

Luke 2:1–14 (15–20)

IN PREPARATION FOR WORSHIP

Your grace appears in a child to me,
your peace in vulnerability.
I will set aside all my fear,
I will summon all my inner joy,
I will lift my heart for heaven to hear,
and worship you in this little boy.

CALL TO WORSHIP

Sing, O people! Sing, O earth!
Sing to the LORD a new song!
> **Great is the LORD, and greatly to be praised!**
> **Let us tell of God's salvation every day!**
Ascribe, O people, ascribe, O earth,
Ascribe to the LORD glory and strength!
> **Great is the LORD, who alone has made the heavens!**
> **Let us declare God's glory among the nations!**
Rejoice, O heavens! Rejoice, O earth!
Let the seas and trees, the forests and fields rejoice, for the LORD is coming!

> **Great is the LORD, and holy is God's name!**
> **Let us worship our God in holy splendor!**

OPENING PRAYER

Saving God, the light of your love has shined upon us, the light of your Son, Jesus Christ, who is born for our hope and salvation! So scatter the darkness of this sinful world with the brilliance of your glory, that the nations might assemble under your rule of peace! So increase the honor of your holy name, that every creature under heaven might worship with us the holy Christ child, and proclaim him Wonderful Counselor, Prince of Peace!

CALL TO CONFESSION

God will judge the people with equity, the world with righteousness and truth! For Christ has been born to bring us peace, and has given himself on our behalf to redeem us from all sin and to purify us from all iniquity. Let us confess to God all our sinful ways and relinquish them. For this reason Christ was born: to be our Savior and to be our Lord.

PRAYER OF CONFESSION

God of Glory, we confess that our lives are choked and crowded with the competing idols of our culture and the persistence of our worldly passions. We have reserved only the humblest room for you. We are unworthy to serve as hosts of your holy goodness. Forgive us, remove our sin, and remain with us, that we might welcome you into our fallen world and adore you as our precious, perfect guest.

DECLARATION OF FORGIVENESS

The grace of God has appeared to us in Jesus, bringing salvation to all! Even as we wait for the blessed hope and the manifestation of God's glory, let us together renounce impiety and live godly lives in accordance with the will of Jesus Christ, our Savior, in whom we are forgiven!

PRESENTATION OF TITHES AND OFFERINGS

In bearing the Christ as a child for us, God has given us cause for celebration, the LORD has increased our joy! How can we express appropriate joy unless we receive the Son of God into our hearts? How can we worthily celebrate God's self-giving unless we also give of ourselves?

Prayer of Dedication

Glory to God in the highest heaven! You, O God, are great and true, wonderful and mighty, eternal and eternally gracious to us, for the gift you have given for our salvation comes not in a package or a principle, a law or a concept, but in a baby born to us. We thank you with these finite gifts for your infinite goodness to us, and we ask you to bless them for your use in bringing your good tidings of great joy to all the people, in Jesus' holy and precious name.

The Blessing

Carry the Spirit of Christ with you, not only at Christmas, but throughout the year! Return to God in weekly worship, and partake of the peace of God's holy rest! Serve the LORD with good deeds each day, and when Christ returns, he will know you!

Christmas, Second Proper (ABC)
Christmas Morning

Isaiah 62:6–12

Psalm 97

Titus 3:4–7

Luke 2:(1–7) 8–20

In Preparation for Worship

O Blessed One, you have appeared to us in the quiet glory
of a holy child come to save us, born to set us free.
Gather us into the hopeful dawn
of your marvelous new creation, that we might be
born anew in the light of your Son as we recall the sacred story.

Call to Worship

Let the heavens sing out in praise of God's righteousness!
Our salvation comes in Christ Jesus our Lord,
by the mercy, the goodness, and the lovingkindness of our God!
Let the good news ring out to the ends of the earth!
Our salvation comes with great reward,
for God will grant us the fruit of our labors!
Let all the peoples behold the glory of God!
Our salvation comes! We are not forsaken!
Our Redeeming God has sought us out!

Opening Prayer

Sovereign Lord, your light has dawned upon the righteous and your joy for the upright in heart! As we consider the holy Christ child and treasure him in our hearts, grant to each of us the washing of rebirth and renewal by the Holy Spirit, that we might be born in him and he in us. Raise us up into new spheres of joy, where we shall sing with all the hosts of heaven, "Glory to God in the highest heaven, and on earth peace among those whom the Lord favors!"

Call to Confession

The Lord loves those who hate evil. God rescues them from the hand of the wicked. Let us hasten to register our hatred of evil and forsake the sin that is in us. In confession, let us surrender our sins to God's consuming fire.

Prayer of Confession

Righteous God, we confess that we have bowed to worthless idols, needless pressures, unholy desires, and unreasonable demands. How can these compare with your Holy Spirit and your saving Son? Forgive us, O God, for our misdirected worship. Lead us to the manger once again, that we may adore you with reverent love, grateful joy, and humble simplicity.

Declaration of Forgiveness

The heart of the gospel is that God has saved us, not according to any good works we have done, but according to the steadfast and loving mercy of the Lord. We are washed, reborn, renewed by the Holy Spirit, who is poured out upon us richly in Christ Jesus, so that having been justified by grace, we might become heirs with Jesus according to the hope of eternal life. This saying is sure. Therefore, have joy and be at peace! In Christ we are not only forgiven, we are destined to live eternally with our Lord in everlasting joy!

Presentation of Tithes and Offerings

True worship of the Christ means that we find our Lord worth not only our love, our obedience, and our praise, but also worth infinitely more than our treasures and our gifts. Let us invest ourselves, along with our tithes and offerings, in building this missionary outpost of the government of God.

Prayer of Dedication

O Lord, you have sworn that your people shall not be overrun by your enemies, but that the faithful shall eat and drink the fruits of their own harvest! As we thank you for your plentiful blessings, please honor our rendering of these your gifts, that they might join your outward flow of mercies, reach and touch those who need them, and give all credit and praise to the name of Jesus!

The Blessing

Go forth humbly, with the Christ child reigning over your life! Go forth joyfully, praising God in all circumstances, full of the Holy Spirit and the hope of eternal life! Go forth in song, giving glory to the Lord for the marvelous thing that has taken place. And may God, the holy Trinity, guard you, guide you, keep and preserve you for the kingdom of heaven, this holy day and for all time to come!

Christmas, Third Proper (ABC)

Christmas Day

Isaiah 52:7–10

Psalm 98

Hebrews 1:1–4 (5–12)

John 1:1–14

IN PREPARATION FOR WORSHIP

O you who are above the angels,
you who command them as the wind
and your servants like flame:
your image is perfect, your glory excels!
We bow to praise your holy name!
We bow to praise your holy name!

CALL TO WORSHIP

Lift up your voices and sing for joy!
> **The good news is heard! Salvation has come!**

Break forth together in joyful song!
> **The glory of the LORD has returned to Zion!**

How beautiful are those who herald God's peace!
> **Our God reigns! Our God reigns!**

OPENING PRAYER

Creator God, you are the maker of heaven and earth! You contain your whole creation, for you are eternal and LORD of all! Though the world wears out, you will remain! Though the firmament be folded up and put away, you are the same forever! Your years will have no end!

Call to Confession

The One who loves righteousness and hates wickedness is full of grace and truth. Sinners find no more honest and merciful judge than the Word of God made flesh. If anyone understands our trials and temptations, it is Jesus Christ, who gives to those who trust in him the right to become children of God! Let us entrust our confession to the One whose name is truth!

Prayer of Confession

Holy and Eternal God, forgive us, for we are ever confusing the messenger with the message, the angelic herald with the holy Word. We saddle your servants with our selfish expectations, and tear them down when they fail to deliver. Reveal our idolatries, and pardon each one, that we may focus anew on your perfection. Restore us to rightful worship of the Christ who reigns with you over all creation!

Declaration of Forgiveness

Jesus Christ has made purification for sins and is seated at the right hand of God's majesty on high! Darkness cannot overcome the light of Jesus! Death cannot prevail against the life that Christ gives! Sin cannot conquer those who are forgiven according to the fullness of God's grace! Claim the saving benefits of the grace that God has shown you, and be at peace with yourselves, with one another, and with the Lord!

Presentation of Tithes and Offerings

Christ is the appointed heir of all things, through whom God created the worlds! This One who reigns over heaven and earth openly shares with us the teeming blessings of grace. Let us now participate in this divine act of sharing, in the holy name of the Most High!

Prayer of Dedication

God of Grace and Truth, you have sent your Word, Jesus Christ, into the world, which belongs entirely to him. As we open our hearts to receive the holy child, help us also open our hands in love. Move us to be generous as you are generous. Make us gracious as Christ is gracious. Bless this offering with the grace of your Holy Spirit, for it is in Jesus' name that we present it to you.

THE BLESSING

Go forth from this place and bear witness to the light of Christ!
Testify to the Word of God, that all might come to believe!
Obey the leadings of the Holy Spirit, that your lives may be filled with joy!

First Sunday after Christmas

Isaiah 61:10—62:3

Psalm 148

Galatians 4:4–7

Luke 2:22–40

In Preparation for Worship

Praise to you, O Holy Splendor!
For you have robed me for the presentation,
clothed me with garments of salvation,
chosen this child for your sanctuary!
Praise to you, O Holy Splendor!
Your eternal beauty dwells within!

Call to Worship

Rejoice in the Lord with exceeding joy!
Do not keep silent, but exult in the Lord!
>   **Salvation shines forth like a burning torch!**
>   **Victory breaks out like a new day dawning!**
The nations shall see the glory of God's people!
All creation shall see it and praise the Lord!
>   **Our God has called righteousness forth!**
>   **The praises of the Lord arise from the earth!**
Open your hearts to the Spirit of Christ!
Let the light of God stream through you!
>   **The glory of the Lord is alive and among us!**
>   **The Lord has come to redeem us!**

Opening Prayer

O Divine Master, you have promised consolation for your chosen people, and a wonderful inheritance for your adopted children! Help us to trust in your marvelous grace, to know your peace, and to respond with lives of devotion and reverence, for in Christ Jesus, you have welcomed us into your family and chosen us to share in your heavenly blessings!

Call to Confession

Our future is not one of enslavement, but one of freedom, not one of childishness, but one of adoption as children who will come of age and inherit the kingdom of God with Christ! Let us leave our former ways behind us in confession.

Prayer of Confession

Saving God, we step into your revealing light, knowing that not all of our inner thoughts are godly, not all of our deeds holy, not all of our words worthy. Examine us, that the truths you would have us know about ourselves might pierce our hearts, renew our minds, and quicken our souls. Purify us, that your Holy Spirit might give growth to your children, in the name of Jesus Christ.

Declaration of Forgiveness

Children of God, be joyful! The Lord has worked vindication for you! You shall be given a new name, a crown of beauty, and a radiant glory, for you are not only forgiven, but you are legitimate members of God's own family. Be cheerful, hopeful, grateful, and kind, for the rich favor by which you are redeemed and adopted in Christ Jesus!

Presentation of Tithes and Offerings

As the holy family presented the Christ child in the temple and came to offer their gifts for purification in accordance with the law of Moses, let us also offer ourselves along with our gifts, trusting that, in doing so, we might be made ever more pure of heart, ever more encouraged to serve our God, and ever more invested in the glorious reign of Christ Jesus over heaven and earth.

PRAYER OF DEDICATION

Gracious God, you have faithfully provided for us from age to age! With joy and thanksgiving we lift up to you, for you to bless, these humble expressions of our reverence and devotion! With them we also present to you the holy child born within each of us, asking that you would fill us with his wisdom, strengthen us for his service, and grow us in his likeness, that our lives might show forth his glory to the world.

THE BLESSING

Now may the LORD dismiss you with peace,
may the Word dwell with you,
may the Holy Spirit rest upon you,
for the light of revelation is shining for all people,
and you are bearers of that holy light!

Second Sunday after Christmas (ABC)

Jeremiah 31:7–14

Psalm 147:12–20

Ephesians 1:3–14

John 1:(1–9) 10–18

IN PREPARATION FOR WORSHIP

O God, you have blessed us
with every spiritual blessing under heaven.
O Christ, in you we have found our purpose.
O Spirit, your promise is our inheritance of redemption.
Blessed are you, Giver of Light.
May our worship glorify you!

CALL TO WORSHIP

The Son is born, the beloved of God!
Through adoption,
we too are heirs of all things with Christ.
Jesus Christ is the Light,
the Light no darkness can overcome.
So shall we be a light to the nations!
Christ is our hope and salvation.
So shall we live to praise God's glory!

OPENING PRAYER

Eternal Word, we have sensed your invisible light shining in the darkness.
We have heard your unspeakable Word in our hearts. We stand before

you in wonder, for you have called us here, out of sin, reached us in the distant throes of loneliness and wanting, and drawn us into your holy purpose. We await your instruction. We await your command.

Call to Confession

God's Word came into the world, full of grace and truth. The truth is that we are sinners, once lost in the darkness of this world. The grace is that Christ's purpose is to atone for sin, to embody God's forgiveness, to call everyone into the eternal light of God's love. The more willing we are to admit this truth, the deeper our appreciation of God's overwhelming grace in Jesus Christ, the Word of God. Let us confess our sins.

Prayer of Confession

O Blessed God, you have called your people to be holy and blameless, yet we admit we are tainted by sin, guilty of succumbing to human will and the desires of the flesh. You have come to your own, yet we have not known you fully. Forgive us, and give us the power to be your children, alive to your truth, responsive to your will.

Declaration of Forgiveness

The Lord has promised to turn mourning into joy, sorrow into comfort and gladness! As the Lord has ransomed Israel, so Christ has ransomed a world of sinners from enemies too strong for us to resist on our own. We are redeemed through the blood of Christ, according to the riches of grace which God has lavished upon us. Therefore, let your hearts be still, and give thanks to God.

Presentation of Tithes and Offerings

We are heirs of God's blessings through Christ: forgiven of our sins, sealed with the promised Holy Spirit, adopted as children of God, with every spiritual blessing! How shall we use our blessings? Surely in thanksgiving to God, for the rich inheritance that we have received through Christ Jesus!

PRAYER OF DEDICATION

Your good pleasure, we are told, is to gather all things to yourself, things in heaven and things on earth. Therefore we offer you these things, and ourselves as living sacrifices, expressions of praise to you, that your glory might be increased, and your goodness celebrated by all people.

THE BLESSING

You have been given grace upon grace!
Therefore, be filled with the Spirit, born of God,
and bearers of the living Word, Jesus Christ.

Epiphany (ABC)

Isaiah 60:1–6

Psalm 72:1–7, 10–14

Ephesians 3:1–12

Matthew 2:1–12

In Preparation for Worship

Holy Child of God,
we have sought you from afar.
Receive us as we bring you worship.
Welcome us into your quiet presence.
Gather all who would present themselves to you,
that every stranger might become your friend.

Call to Worship

Arise and shine; for your light has come
and the glory of the LORD has risen upon you.
>Thick darkness covered us and all the earth.
>But the LORD has arisen upon us.

Lift up your eyes and look around.
See how the nations come from far away.
>We have followed the light to this holy place.
>We gather in the dawning of the light of God.

Look and be radiant!
Let your hearts rejoice!
>We bring the wealth of many nations,
>All to praise our glorious God.

Opening Prayer

Self-revealing God, you have entered into our human world so that righteousness will flourish and peace abound. We gather to offer you our hearts for worship, our mouths for praise, our hands for humble service. May you meet us here so that your light within us might increase, and your justice might be done.

Call to Confession

We have access to God in boldness and confidence through the faith we have in Jesus Christ, and if our own faith is lacking, we have Christ to have faith for us. Therefore, there is no place to hide our sin from the Lord, no reason not to have courage in Christ. Let us boldly confess our sins to God, and our earnest desire to repent and be healed.

Prayer of Confession

Light of the World, you pierce the darkness. Penetrate the darkness in our hearts. We hold in the light of your glory all the sins that we have known, all the pain that we have caused, all that causes us regret. We pray that, in your mercy and your love, you would once again forgive our sin, remove it from us, and transform us in your holy light, so that we might draw ever nearer to you, for your name's sake.

Declaration of Forgiveness

God is a responsive God: saving those who cry out in need, helping those who have no help, showing mercy to the weak, redeeming those oppressed by violence. Know that God has heard your prayer. Grace is given to all the saints, from the least to the greatest, so that all might share in the boundless riches of Christ. In Jesus Christ, you are forgiven.

Presentation of Tithes and Offerings

The mystery of God's plan from the beginning is revealed: In Jesus Christ we are all one body, born in purity, guided by law, empowered by grace, crucified by sin, buried in baptism, raised in glory. Since we share in everything with Christ, let us care for the Church, his body, by offering our gifts to God.

PRAYER OF DEDICATION

As wise ones rendered you the gift of gold, we dedicate our wealth to you. As they offered you fragrant incense, we send up to you each thought as prayer. As they gave you a healing balm, we ask that you would use these offerings to heal the wounded, the weak, and the broken, through our common ministry in Christ.

THE BLESSING

Do not return by the way that you came.
The path is new that lies before you.
Do not forget the light that leads you.
The light is eternal that guides your steps.
Do not fail to give thanks for the joy,
for the child, the Christ, who is born in you.

First Sunday after Epiphany
Ordinary Time 1 (*Baptism of the Lord*)

Genesis 1:1–5

Psalm 29

Acts 19:1–7

Mark 1:4–11

IN PREPARATION FOR WORSHIP

Come down, O God of glory!
Come down, O humble Christ!
Come down, O baptizing Spirit!
Spill into every nation, every land, every heart, every mind.
Make us one with you and with all your chosen ones.

CALL TO WORSHIP

In the beginning, the Spirit of God was moving over the chaos waters.
   As Jesus was coming up out of the water,
   the Spirit of God came down.
In the beginning, the earth was a formless void,
and darkness was over the face of the deep.
   The heavens opened, and a voice said:
   You are my beloved Son.
In the beginning, God said, "Let there be light!" And there was light.
   O LORD, we have been baptized with water.
   Now baptize us with the Holy Spirit.

Opening Prayer

Maker of Light, you have separated light from darkness, and torn the sky in two for the Dove of heaven to descend. Rest with favor upon us, we pray, that we might know your blessing, employ our tongues and talents to your glory, and extend the wonderful news of Jesus Christ to every creature in every corner of the world.

Call to Confession

Even the sinless one, Jesus Christ, submitted to baptism, which marks our lives by a dying to sin, a death in which we are made one with Christ. Therefore, let us confess our sin, joining our sins with him in his death on the cross, so that Jordan's waters might also carry our sins away to the Dead Sea.

Prayer of Confession

Creator Spirit, your waters are deep and wide enough to baptize the whole world. The star by which you led the wise men was bright enough for all to see. Yet we confess we love with a narrow love, a love that feels safest and surest among our own. Forgive us, Lord. Invade us with your sanctifying Spirit, that we might love with an ever greater and ever purer love.

Declaration of Forgiveness

In our dying to sin, we have died with Christ. But Christ's death is both a death to sin, and the death of sin. When Christ took on the sins of the world, sin died with him on the cross. But Christ was also raised up from the water as from the grave. He it is who leads us through the waters and into eternal life. Friends, to the extent that we are alive in Christ, we are indeed forgiven and free from sin.

Presentation of Tithes and Offerings

In the joyous freedom of baptismal surrender, in gazing upon the precious Christ child, we can see that nothing we would withhold from God can compare with the invaluable treasure we have in heaven, a treasure we gain by forsaking earthly rewards. Let nothing prevent you from giving to the LORD the very best you have to offer.

PRAYER OF DEDICATION

God of epiphanies, though we recognize your presence sporadically and inconsistently, yet your mission and the needs of this world do not relent, and your kingdom does not sleep. Receive these gifts that your mission might be sustained in us, among us, and through us. Make them holy and inspire us in their use, that we might be ever faithful, and ever diligent in making your will and purpose known to others.

THE BLESSING

The Spirit of God goes with the pure in heart.
May your hearts be free of every evil and full of love.
The voice of God speaks, and all cry "Glory!"
May the Word of God be on your lips,
telling the good news of grace in Christ.
The Creator of heaven and earth is enthroned forever.
May God be in your hearts and grant you peace.

Second Sunday after Epiphany
Ordinary Time 2

1 Samuel 3:1–10 (11–20)

Psalm 139:1–6, 13–18

1 Corinthians 6:12–20

John 1:43–51

IN PREPARATION FOR WORSHIP

O Lord, you know my every thought,
my every movement, my every way;
search me and oversee me,
that I might know your constant presence
and be with you to the end.

CALL TO WORSHIP

You are not your own! But anyone united to the LORD
is one with Christ in the Spirit!
    Come, O Spirit, to your holy temple!
You have been bought with a price!
Therefore, glorify God in your body!
    Come, O Spirit, to your holy temple!
God has raised the Lord Jesus from death,
and will raise us also with Christ!
    Welcome, O Spirit, to your holy temple!
    We open our hearts to you!

Opening Prayer

We praise you, O God, for you have seen and known us, even before you called us. Open up your heavens, Lord, that we may behold and glorify your Son and our Savior, Jesus Christ, in whose name we pray.

Call to Confession

The LORD knows when you sit and when you stand. God knows your thoughts from far away, even before you speak them. You cannot escape or hide from God. What alternative have you, then, but to trust the one whose hand is upon you, who knit you in your mother's womb, who formed your inward being? Let us trust the God who knows us best with all that we truly are, with all that we have done, and with all that we have failed to do.

Prayer of Confession

Creator God, you have formed our bodies for your purposes and you seek to dwell within us. Yet we confess that we have used our bodies for sin, wronging both the sacred temple you have given us and doing harm to those around us, including your body, the Church. We ask your forgiveness, inviting you to search each of us, inside and out, to cleanse us, and to make us once again a suitable dwelling for your Holy Spirit, in Jesus' name.

Declaration of Forgiveness

God has raised the Lord Jesus from death, and God will also raise us by the power of the Holy Spirit! For Jesus Christ has purchased us, at the cost of his own life. Therefore, you are no longer your own, but you belong to Christ, in whom you are free and freely forgiven.

Presentation of Tithes and Offerings

Let there be no deceit among us. The LORD is acquainted with all our ways. The whole of life is open to God's view. In the sight of God and in the fellowship of this spiritual body, let us open our hearts and our hands in the very public act of giving in the name of our Lord Jesus Christ.

PRAYER OF DEDICATION

Wonderful are your works and your knowledge, O God! For you have created and blessed us. May our lives be lived entirely in you; may our hearts overflow with love for you; may the works of our hands and these gifts we lift up to you bear fruit for your kingdom and glorify your holy name.

THE BLESSING

Listen for God in the quiet of the night.
Look for Jesus Christ in the full light of day.
Attend to the Word and follow the Spirit,
and you will see and hear and speak and do
great little things for the kingdom of God.

Third Sunday after Epiphany
Ordinary Time 3

Jonah 3:1–5, 10

Psalm 62:5–12

1 Corinthians 7:29–31

Mark 1:14–20

IN PREPARATION FOR WORSHIP

God of the prophets,
you have called us to repentance;
therefore, we turn to you.
You have called us to follow you;
therefore, we lay down our nets and come.
You have challenged us to fish for people;
therefore, we lift heart and voice to you in praise,
open our arms unto the world, and wait.

CALL TO WORSHIP

Trust in God at all times, O people;
In all things, pour out your hearts to the LORD!
   God is our rock!
   The LORD alone is our mighty refuge!
The lowly are but a breath, the proud a delusion.
Trust not in the things of this world.
   To the LORD alone belong power and glory!
   To God alone belongs steadfast love!

Trust not in ill-gotten gains.
If your riches increase do not set your heart on them.
Let us set our hearts on God alone.
All our hopes are on the LORD!
Let us wait, O people, let us wait for the LORD.
God repays all according to their work.
Therefore, let us worship our righteous God!

OPENING PRAYER

God of the Journey, we have heard your summons and we praise you for it. We follow you, seeking your purpose for our lives. We come to you, asking where you will lead us. We come listening for your message to us as we journey through this troubled world. Speak to us. Lead us. Reveal to us our destiny along the way.

CALL TO CONFESSION

The time is short! The present form of this world is passing away! Take your leave of anything and everything that hinders your devotion to the LORD. Turn to the LORD! Put God before all else, and know that the kingdom of God has come very near. Repent of your sins; confess and surrender them to the LORD.

PRAYER OF CONFESSION

God of the good news, we confess to you that we occupy our hands with fruitless tasks, our minds with distractions, our time with diversions. Our superficial flurry is but a thin disguise covering our spiritual slug-gishness. How often have we actually abandoned our nets, followed you in faith, and testified to your kingdom? Forgive us, and renew your life in us so that we might be your willing and responsive servants, in Jesus' name.

DECLARATION OF FORGIVENESS

You have heard the call to faith and humbled yourselves before the LORD. Now be filled with the Holy Spirit! God has chosen you to receive forgive-ness, to be holy servants of the kingdom of heaven. Therefore, proclaim the saving grace and goodness of Jesus Christ to those who do not know the LORD.

PRESENTATION OF TITHES AND OFFERINGS

All power, love, and mercy belong to God, who repays to everyone according to their work. Set not your heart on riches, but offer your heart and your riches to God, to whom everything belongs, to whom everything eventually returns.

PRAYER OF DEDICATION

Our hope is in you and in you alone, O God, for you are ever doing great deeds with small things. Though we ourselves are but a breath and the gifts we give but a small reflection of our love for you, nevertheless, we trust you to do a great thing with this offering, that your holy name might be praised by those who witness your marvelous works.

THE BLESSING

The kingdom of God is near at hand,
so devote all your loyalties to God!
The way of Christ lies before you,
so cast down your nets and follow Jesus!
The voice of the Spirit will guide your steps,
so invest all your trust in the LORD!

Fourth Sunday after Epiphany
Ordinary Time 4

Deuteronomy 18:15–20

Psalm 111

1 Corinthians 8:1–13

Mark 1:21–28

IN PREPARATION FOR WORSHIP

Holy Spirit of God, you reign over all creation,
you command even the unclean spirits
and they obey you.
Make us clean
and ready for worship.
Make us obedient to no lesser spirit,
to a spirit no less holy than that of your Son, Jesus Christ.

CALL TO WORSHIP

There is One God, the Creator of all,
in whom we live and move and have our being.
There is One Lord, Jesus Christ,
for whom and through whom all things were made.
There are many spirits, but there is only One Holy Spirit.
All who love God are known by Him,
who puts his Spirit upon and within his people.
Let us worship God.

OPENING PRAYER

Self-giving God, in Jesus Christ we see your goodness at work: teaching with authority, silencing demons, casting out unholiness, manifesting the coming kingdom in the here and now. In his suffering with us and in his suffering for us, Jesus has made us aware of, and alive to, your winsome grace. Therefore, we praise you, with your new creation, inviting you into the deep center of our lives, for your glory and for our continued transformation into the likeness of Christ.

CALL TO CONFESSION

Many are the demons that seek to possess us, and many the idols we possess. Yet, even the demons recognize and confess that Jesus is the Holy One, the Son of the Most High God. How are we different from them? As the baptized, it is appointed to us to repeatedly turn away from sin, to renounce evil and its ways in the world, and to faithfully seek Christ—not with fear, as the demons do, but with trust in God's quickness to forgive. Let us confess our sins.

PRAYER OF CONFESSION

Saving Lord, your holy word exposes us; we see ourselves as we truly are, as in a mirror. We confess our sins, all our sad, particular failings, though it is our inclination to hide them. Help us trust you with them; do away with them as you see fit. Help us trust you with our selves, trust that you will draw us out of our hiding places and reveal the seeds of hope and glory which you have sown within us, even as we step into the transforming light of your amazing love; in Jesus' name we pray.

DECLARATION OF FORGIVENESS

The LORD has sent redemption to the people. God has commanded the old and new covenants, and is ever mindful of our need for forgiveness. The LORD is gracious and merciful, providing Jesus Christ, the bread of life, the true vine, as food and drink for those who fear God and confess their need for salvation. Know that it is for you that Christ has died. It is for you that Christ has risen. It is for you that Christ will come again. I declare to you, in the name of Jesus Christ, you are forgiven.

PRESENTATION OF TITHES AND OFFERINGS

God's desire is not to own or exploit us, but for us to freely give of ourselves, just as Jesus freely gave, and continues to give, of himself, for our joy and salvation. It is this mutual self-giving, to God and from God, in absolute trust, which is pleasing to our LORD.

PRAYER OF DEDICATION

The giftedness of your people testifies to your overflowing grace, even when we need grace to recognize our giftedness. The gratitude of your people testifies to our dependence upon you, even to give you adequate expressions of thanks. Touch this offering with your creative, cleansing hand, that our modest means might yet be used to build your eternal kingdom, where every sin is forgotten, every tear is wiped away, and the glory of your holy name will shine forever.

THE BLESSING

You are a blessed people, holy unto the LORD.
You are fed by the Word of God.
Now be filled with the Holy Spirit.
Go, therefore, and live in holiness, love with compassion,
and give no quarter to evil as you seek always to live in Christ.

Fifth Sunday after Epiphany
Ordinary Time 5

Isaiah 40:21–31

Psalm 147:1–11, 20c

1 Corinthians 9:16–23

Mark 1:29–39

IN PREPARATION FOR WORSHIP

I seek you in a desert place,
far from all distractions and demands.
I seek you in the morning,
in the silence of the waking dawn.
I seek you in the dark interior,
in the infinite reserve of your renewal.

CALL TO WORSHIP

Have you not known? Have you not heard?
The LORD is the everlasting God, the Creator of all the earth!
>   **God gives power to the faint and strength to the weak.**
>   **Praise the LORD!**
Has it not been told you from the beginning?
It is God who stretches out the heavens
and makes the rulers of the earth as nothing!
>   **God does not faint or grow weary.**
>   **Who is equal to the LORD?**
Even youths will faint and be weary.
The young will fall down exhausted.

But those who wait for the LORD shall renew their strength.
They shall mount up with wings like eagles.

OPENING PRAYER

O God, who heals the brokenhearted and binds up their wounds, who lifts up the downtrodden and casts the wicked to the ground: we praise your gracious goodness, your power and understanding. We thank you that you care for us. We hope in your steadfast love.

CALL TO CONFESSION

The time is short. Scarcely do we begin life, take root, and grow, when the wind blows and we wither and are carried away. Who can save us but the very God who created us? Let us confess our sin to our gracious and everlasting God.

PRAYER OF CONFESSION

We confess to you, Healing God, that we are sick of the sin we carry in ourselves, the sin that still plagues your Church and every corner of this fallen world. Even our best efforts are frustrated and exhausted by our own sin and the sins of those around us. You alone sit above the earth and have the power to make us new. Banish every evil impulse within us. Heal us and lift us up. Separate us from all our sins and save us from their consequences, in Jesus' name!

DECLARATION OF FORGIVENESS

As the LORD builds up Jerusalem and gathers the outcasts of Israel, so Jesus comes to heal the sick, cast out demons, and share the suffering of the brokenhearted. By Christ's wounds, our wounds are healed. By the grace of our Lord, we are forgiven.

PRESENTATION OF TITHES AND OFFERINGS

It is God who has fed us from the beginning, who prepares rain for all the earth, who makes the grass to grow on the hills. It is God who is great and gracious, whose power is abundant, and whose understanding is beyond measure. Let us praise the LORD with our offerings of thanks.

PRAYER OF DEDICATION

Merciful God, you have given us freedom and commissioned us with the responsibility for sharing the gospel, free of charge, with people in all walks of life. Give us courage and humility to become all things to all people, and to use these gifts in accordance with your will, all for the sake of the spreading of your Word!

THE BLESSING

May the God who meets you at every turn
heal and renew you with the Holy Spirit,
proclaim in you the glory of Jesus Christ,
and lift you up in the silent presence of your Creator.

Sixth Sunday after Epiphany / Proper 1
Ordinary Time 6

2 Kings 5:1–14

Psalm 30

1 Corinthians 9:24–27

Mark 1:40–45

IN PREPARATION FOR WORSHIP

Keep us from aimless wanderings, Lord!
Direct us along your way.
Bathe us with your healing Word.
Fill us with your Spirit! Fit us for this race!

CALL TO WORSHIP

Sing praises to the LORD, O people of faith!
Give thanks to God's holy name!
 We will not be silent, but we will praise the LORD.
 O LORD our God, we will give thanks to you forever!
God has drawn us up from the pit!
The LORD has restored us, that we might give praise!
 When I cried to you, O LORD, you healed me.
 You have not let my enemies triumph over me!
Weeping may linger for the night,
But joy comes with the morning!
 You have turned my mourning into dancing!
 Therefore, I will praise you as long as I live!

OPENING PRAYER

Merciful God, you offer us such great rewards for simply trusting and keeping faith with you! Let this be our worship of your holiness, that we might be charged with the good news of your saving power, alive with the joy of your Holy Spirit, and disciplined in the service of your glory!

CALL TO CONFESSION

The healing hand of the LORD is available to drive out disease, sickness, and sin, and to restore us to health, life, and wholeness. Do not let God's anger at human sin keep you from asking for the cleansing that you need, for the mercy of the LORD is forever! Let us make our appeal to our saving God.

PRAYER OF CONFESSION

Most High and Holy God, how is it that we lack so much self-control? We waste our energies seeking perishable rewards, and give little thought to the imperishable ones. We are often too proud to accept your humble solutions, too vain to practice simple self-discipline. Cleanse us, LORD, and correct us! Set us on a new course of obedience and faith, that we might be of greater service to you, in Jesus' name.

DECLARATION OF FORGIVENESS

The anger of the LORD is but for a moment, but the favor of the LORD is for a lifetime! Take off your sackcloth and be clothed with joy! Let all who cry to the LORD be healed, restored, renewed, and forgiven! Christ has given us the cleansing we need! Therefore, give praise to your healing God, and proclaim to the world the goodness of our LORD!

PRESENTATION OF TITHES AND OFFERINGS

The LORD establishes us in times of properity and answers us in times of woe. We cannot ask for a more faithful God than the One whom we worship and serve. For the ultimate gift is not simply to be saved, but to confirm our salvation by participating in God's reconciling work in Christ Jesus, that others might be saved by Christ through our imitation of Christ. Therefore, let us rededicate ourselves and offer our gifts to this end!

Prayer of Dedication

Holy One, you do such great things in such quiet ways, not for any compensation but only for a sacrifice of thanks and joy and praise! We would learn from you, our gracious Creator, from your self-giving Christ, from your Spirit of wisdom, that we might be pleasing to you as we participate in your saving work. Bless these gifts, then, that they might be used to bless others in your holy name!

The Blessing

Go in freedom from all that would harm you,
and freely proclaim salvation in Christ!
Go with joy in the Spirit of life,
and joyfully share your spiritual gifts!
Go in peace, for God is at work in you;
so work for the LORD with deep consolation!

Seventh Sunday after Epiphany / Proper 2
Ordinary Time 7

Isaiah 43:18–25

Psalm 41

2 Corinthians 1:18–22

Mark 2:1–12

IN PREPARATION FOR WORSHIP

Everlasting God,
whose every promise is affirmed in Christ Jesus,
pour your Holy Spirit into my heart
and into the hearts of all those here gathered,
for the world conspires to empty us of faith,
and without you we can only languish!

CALL TO WORSHIP

Let those whom God has established in Christ
receive the gift of the Holy Spirit in their hearts!
    Seal, O Christ, with your sign of promise
    all who say "Amen!" to the glory of God!
Let those whom the LORD has formed into a people
declare the praise of the Creator God!
    In Christ, every one of God's promises is "Yes!"
    Jesus, our LORD, has authority to save!
Let those to whom God has given the gospel of forgiveness
tell the world of the mercies of the LORD!

Truly, the glory of the LORD is with us!
Truly, our God is about to do a new thing!

OPENING PRAYER

Our Holy God and Guide, who carves paths through the impassable wilderness and makes rivers flow in the desert, we seek your presence, we thirst for you. You alone can lead us to safety. You alone can satisfy. You alone are worthy of all honor and glory and praise!

CALL TO CONFESSION

Have we not burdened God with our sins? Have we not worn the LORD out with our iniquities? Beloved, God is eager to do a new thing! Therefore, let us sacrifice the old patterns of sin, submit to the creative judgment of our gracious God, and thereby honor Jesus Christ with our honest confession.

PRAYER OF CONFESSION

O LORD, be gracious to us and heal us, for we have sinned against you and against one another. We have wasted opportunities in fear of failure, wasted energies in fruitless pursuits, and wasted resources in thoughtless excesses. We have failed to call upon you as you would have us do. Do not let evil triumph over us, O God. Blot out our transgressions for the sake of your name and your new creation, that we might honor you with right sacrifices and declare your praise!

DECLARATION OF FORGIVENESS

The all-knowing God has pledged not to remember your sins, but the LORD has given you the Holy Spirit in your hearts as a first installment, a guarantee of your eternal salvation, that you might live for the praise of the glory of God! Therefore, take heart, for your sins are forgiven! Have faith, for you are established in the grace of God! Walk uprightly, for your integrity and your authority come from the LORD!

PRESENTATION OF TITHES AND OFFERINGS

Happy are those who consider the weak and the poor! The LORD delivers them in the day of trouble. Blessed are those who walk with integrity, for they will stand in God's presence forever! Let us offer our gifts in thanksgiving to our blessed and everlasting God.

PRAYER OF DEDICATION

Gracious God, we would honor you with our gifts. Therefore, we lift them up in devotion to you, for you withhold nothing good from us, you satisfy us and sustain us with every good thing, even with the promise of fullness in this life and in the life to come. Sanctify your servants and these gifts for your service.

THE BLESSING

Open your eyes to perceive the LORD's newness.
Claim the authority of the seal of Christ.
Open your hearts to the flow of the Spirit
and walk in the love of God!

Eighth Sunday after Epiphany / Proper 3
Ordinary Time 8

Hosea 2:14–20

Psalm 103:1–13, 22

2 Corinthians 3:1–6

Mark 2:13–22

IN PREPARATION FOR WORSHIP

O God of our Joy,
you call us to be bearers of your new wine!
So fill us with your life-giving Spirit
and mature us in the love of Jesus Christ,
that we might be a blessing to you
and show forth your worth,
O Giver of Joy!

CALL TO WORSHIP

Come with confidence to the LORD your God!
Be encouraged through Christ who has entered your hearts!
> Let each and every soul bless the LORD!
> Let no one forget the great benefits of knowing God!
Approach the Holy One in the Spirit of worship!
Be open to the outpouring of God's new revelation!
> Let each sinner abandon the former ways!
> Let those who would be saved obey the summons of the LORD!
Gather in the name of the only God who can satisfy!

Be attentive to the Living Word of the LORD!
> **Let us bow our lives before the holy, awesome God.**
> **Let us fear the LORD who is gracious and good!**

OPENING PRAYER

God of the new covenant, we have nothing to say to our credit, no competence to claim as our own. But you are our competence, O LORD, and we are your message of Christ, insofar as you would fill us with the Spirit of life and inscribe us deep into the hearts of those to whom we reach out in Jesus' name.

CALL TO CONFESSION

The One who led Israel out of Egypt seeks renewed relations with one and all! The LORD is merciful and gracious, slow to anger and abounding in steadfast love. God will neither accuse us nor be angry with us forever. Fear the LORD and find compassion! Trust the LORD with your confession, who desires to live with you in righteousness, faithfulness, mercy, and love.

PRAYER OF CONFESSION

Healing God, where would we be without your Holy Spirit? We so often become hardened to the sin and the sickness that we see in the world around us and harbor in ourselves. When we seek simple solutions, we are often crushed by the letter of the law, we forget to have compassion, and we miss out on the many joys of life in the Spirit. Forgive us, heal us, redeem us, and refresh us by the renewing power of your Anointed One, Jesus Christ, who keeps company even with outcasts and sinners for the sake of our salvation!

DECLARATION OF FORGIVENESS

The benefits of the LORD are forgiveness and healing, redemption and renewal, satisfaction and, indeed, a coronation of love! God has not dealt with us according to our sins, nor repaid us according to our iniquities. For as high as the heavens are above the earth, so is the steadfast love of the LORD great toward us. As far as the east is from the west, so far has God removed our transgressions from us. Rejoice in God's compassion toward you, and bless the LORD with all your soul!

Presentation of Tithes and Offerings

God would have us waste nothing. Indeed, to every need belongs one of the benefits of the LORD, each in its proper time and place. Let our act of giving be a demonstration of our willingness to be partnered with God in matching these benefits to the needs around us.

Prayer of Dedication

O God our Provider, you alone can make us a hopeful and fruitful people, for you keep covenant with us and show compassion to all who revere you! May your Spirit give new life to us and to our use of these gifts in your name, that your mighty ways and your wonderful works might be made known to more and more people in this generation and in the generations to come.

The Blessing

Follow Jesus to whomever he directs you.
Harbor the Spirit deep in your heart.
Love the LORD with all that is within you,
and bless the LORD with all your soul!

Last Sunday after Epiphany
(*Transfiguration Sunday*)

2 Kings 2:1–12

Psalm 50:1–6

2 Corinthians 4:3–6

Mark 9:2–9

IN PREPARATION FOR WORSHIP

God of Creation, proclaim your Son, the Holy Word;
Light of the World, reveal the glorified Body of Christ;
Spirit of Truth, speak your Light into our hearts,
that we might worship and serve you.

CALL TO WORSHIP

We do not proclaim ourselves.
> **We proclaim Jesus Christ as Lord,**
> **and ourselves as servants of our Lord!**

The One who said, "Let there be light!"
has shone that light into our hearts.
> **Thus we know the glory of God,**
> **and see the face of Jesus Christ.**

Truly, the kingdom of God has come with power!
> **Let us worship God!**

OPENING PRAYER

God of Light and Glory, you shine forth in the gift of your law, in the light
of your prophets, in the transfigured body of Jesus Christ. Speak your

glory into being in us, that we might reflect your heavenly light on earth and enable others to see your holy presence in their lives.

Call to Confession

Holiness does not come naturally to us. It is a gift which we must ask for and receive from God, and practice with spiritual discipline. Even when we encounter rare and wonderful moments of joy and vision, we must not be misled into thinking that we have arrived at holiness. There is always something more we must surrender to the Lord. Bring your sins, all that causes you to stumble, and lay them at the foot of the cross in confession.

Prayer of Confession

Holy God, in grace you have revealed your Son to be our Savior, and the world's only hope for salvation. But we confess that we would often rather control him and enshrine him, at the cost of stopping the Spirit's gift of growth, of resisting the flow of life. Forgive our sinful blindness and heal our willful deafness, that we may perceive your glory in faith, with all our senses redeemed, and live to praise you with reverent adoration; in Jesus' name.

Declaration of Forgiveness

In his bright, heavenly form, Jesus shows us the promise of the resurrection. This is the body of glory which he came to restore to us, which he is determined to share with us, by means of his suffering on the cross, so that we might be forgiven for our sins against God's holiness. Be at peace, knowing that you are forgiven. Let us show our thanks to God, by living lives of worship and faith.

Presentation of Tithes and Offerings

All that we possess, and all that we would guard and protect, is overshadowed by the holy presence of God in our lives. In acknowledgment of God's providential care for us, in gratitude for all the ways in which we are blessed and preserved, let us bring before God that which we would offer for the glory of God's beloved Son and our beloved Lord.

Prayer of Dedication

You overtake us, but you do not take us over. You endow us with your image, but we can scarcely imagine you. You call us to service, but when we come, we find you are already there, serving. Take our images and offerings, O Lord. Make them be what you would have them be, make them do what you would have them do, in service to your kingdom.

The Blessing

May the God of heaven reveal to you the beloved Word within your hearts.
May the Christ of glory reveal in you the kingdom come in power.
May the Spirit of love reveal through you God's glory in your living faith.

PART II

The Paschal Cycle
Lent—Easter—Pentecost

Ash Wednesday (ABC)

Joel 2:1–2, 12–17 OR Isaiah 58:1–12

Psalm 51:1–17

2 Corinthians 5:20b—6:10

Matthew 6:1–6, 16–21

IN PREPARATION FOR WORSHIP

Lord, we have heard and now heed your call.
We return to you,
repenting of all that is not pleasing to you.
Help us now begin the true fast,
seeking your holiness above all else, to your glory.

CALL TO WORSHIP

The LORD has spoken: Return to me with all your hearts!
Let us return to the LORD our God.
The LORD has spoken: Sanctify a fast! Call the people together!
Let us seek the LORD our God.
The LORD speaks: See, now is the acceptable time.
Now is the day of salvation!
Let us worship the LORD our God.

OPENING PRAYER

Saving God, who calls us to be liberated from sin and selfishness, we search for you, knowing that we are mortal and you are the giver of life. We have no confidence in our words and deeds, but only in your grace, mercy, and forgiveness. You alone are our hope, our salvation. Receive us as prodigals come home. Guide us again into the ways of righteousness and responsibility, peace and compassion, that while we live, we might reflect the goodness of your creation.

LITANY OF PENITENCE

God of justice and truth,
you command us to live according to your perfect will,
yet we have followed our own way, living false, frightened, pretentious lives,
and we have benefited from injustices done to others.
Forgive us, O God.
God of peace and love,
you command us to welcome the stranger, the poor, the sick, and the lonely,
yet we have sought our own safety, wealth, health, and comfort,
and we have created dissension, even among our families and friends.
Forgive us, O God.
God of suffering and service,
you command us to live as your servant Son has done,
yet we shy away from pain, shirk responsibility, and pass by the needy.
Forgive us, O God.
For failing to worship you as faithfully as we should,
Lord, have mercy upon us.
For failing to pray as often as we should,
Lord, have mercy upon us.
For doubting and disbelieving in you,
Lord, have mercy upon us.
For seeking solace in worldly goods, in vain pride, in temporal gratifications,
Lord, have mercy upon us.
For arrogant judgments and petty squabbles, cutting remarks and cruelty,
Lord, have mercy upon us.
Do not turn away from us, O God.
Hear our prayers, which we direct to your heart of mercy,
even as we seek to redirect our lives into your paths of righteousness,
for your name's sake.

PRESENTATION OF TITHES AND OFFERINGS

We give what we can in humility, with no fanfare and no grounds for pride. For in giving, we are only doing what we ought, and what we do with our right hand is of no concern to our left. Let us make offerings acceptable to our God.

Prayer of Dedication

All-seeing, all-knowing God, you know what we give in secret, what we think and say and do in the dark. You judge each gift we make, each action we take, by weighing our heart's humility, sincerity, reverence, and gratitude. Accept these gifts, we humbly pray, and draw them to yourself for your good and holy purpose, in Jesus' name.

The Blessing

The LORD awaits, welcomes, and forgives all who return to the ways of righteousness from the waywardness of sin. Therefore, seek the Lord Jesus in all that you do. Discover the kingdom of God in your secret heart. Keep to the way of life eternal, and encourage one another in the Spirit of love.

First Sunday in Lent

Genesis 9:8–17

Psalm 25:1–10

1 Peter 3:18–22

Mark 1:9–15

IN PREPARATION FOR WORSHIP

Christ arising,
Spirit descending,
Creator proclaiming,
receive us into your presence as we seek renewal in you.
Escort us through the wilderness of this world
and lead us to our joyful end.

CALL TO WORSHIP

The same God who sent the flood also gives the rainbow.
> **The same water that washes the world of sin**
> **also refracts the colors of heaven.**

The same Christ who died for us is also now alive in the Spirit.
> **The same Spirit that drove Jesus into the desert**
> **also sees us through our temptations.**

The ways of God are the ways of steadfast love and faithfulness.
> **Let us seek God's ways with worship and discipline,**
> **for in living the ways of God,**
> **there are many wonderful rewards!**

Opening Prayer

Creator God, you are our life, our means of redemption, our hope for the future. You anticipate all our deepest needs, and you have prepared the way for us to follow. Yet that way leads us to the cross upon which Jesus died for our sake, and to the cross which each of us must bear for your sake. Give us strength and courage to persevere through this season of cross-bearing, that we might keep the faith until you come to take us home.

Call to Confession

Jesus' temptation in the wilderness means, for us, a time of cleansing, a season of confession. For while the One we call sinless had no sin to confess for himself, he certainly had a world full of sin to confess on our behalf. The wilderness is the proving ground of our honesty. Let us honestly confess to God that we participate in the sin of the world, the collective sin for which Jesus died, thereby owning our need to be forgiven.

Prayer of Confession

Holy God, by the waters of the flood, by the waters of baptism, you drown the ways of evil in this world. By the testing of Jesus in the desert, you show us that you prevail over the tempter. Yet we have failed to fully trust the guidance of your Spirit in our own lonely, desert times. Thus evil persists in this world by our own fault, fear, and anxiety. Forgive us, O God, and renew our faith, courage, and hope, that our obedience to you might demonstrate your glory to the world, in Jesus' name.

Declaration of Forgiveness

Scripture tells us that the role of baptism in our salvation is not only to wash sin, like dirt, from the body; baptism also acts as "an appeal to God for a good conscience, through the resurrection of Jesus Christ." It marks us as those for whom Christ died, for whom Christ himself appeals to God for grace and forgiveness. The good news of Jesus Christ is this: that the risen Christ himself prays for us, and that the Father, Son, and Holy Spirit are of the same mind, the same grace, and the same purpose. Friends, know that you are forgiven and be at peace.

Presentation of Tithes and Offerings

What will you give to your Creator, who gives you life and leads you in truth? What do you bring to your Savior, who forgets the sins of the humble? How will you thank your Guiding Spirit, who teaches you the ways of steadfast love and faithfulness? Let us make our dearest offerings to God!

Prayer of Dedication

To you, O Lord, we lift our souls. We place our trust in you. No earthly goods can save us, no worldly wealth redeem us. So let these gifts be a reminder of our covenant with you, and let their use be a word to the world that the tempter is defeated and that Jesus Christ is Lord.

The Blessing

May you know the love the Creator has for you.
May you find the strength that the Christ has to give you.
May you feel the presence of the Spirit who escorts you
throughout this season,
throughout this life,
and into eternity.

Second Sunday in Lent

Genesis 17:1–7, 15–16

Psalm 22:23–31

Romans 4:13–25

Mark 8:31–38

In Preparation for Worship

O God, who gives life to the dead,
who calls into being the things that are not,
we hope against hope in you, we believe your promises,
we seek the righteousness that comes through faith
in Jesus Christ our risen Lord.

Call to Worship

Give glory to God, O children of the covenant!
Praise the Lord, O descendants of Abraham!
> **The Lord does not despise the afflicted.**
> **God hears those who cry out in distress.**
Praise the Lord, O seekers of God!
May your hearts live forever!
> **The poor will eat and be satisfied.**
> **All the ends of the earth shall remember and turn to the Lord.**
To God, indeed, shall all bow down!
Even the dead shall worship God!
Therefore, I will live for the Lord!
> **Our children and theirs will know what the Lord has done!**
> **They will tell those yet unborn that God has delivered them.**

Opening Prayer

Eternal God, your promises rest not on your law but on your grace. May we never weaken in faith, but grow ever stronger, knowing that you alone are worthy of our full trust, you alone give life to the dead, and you alone are to be glorified by our dying to self in order to live.

Call to Confession

We cannot save ourselves, but we can look to Christ's dying and rising for us as the promise that we have a Savior greater than ourselves, greater even than death itself. Therefore, let us turn away from our illusions of self-sufficiency and turn to the God who invites us to live for the sake of the gospel that is ever greater than ourselves. Let us confess our sin and take up our crosses in true repentance and faith.

Prayer of Confession

Redeeming God, we admit that we are overwhelmed by human, worldly concerns. We have not set our minds on things divine and heavenly. We diminish ourselves and discount others when we value ourselves more highly than we should. Forgive us of our sin! Do not let us be put to shame! Help us embrace, for the sake of the gospel, whatever losses and whatever gains you will for us, in your divine wisdom and love.

Declaration of Forgiveness

Let your faith be reckoned to you as righteousness on account of Christ, who was handed over to death so that our right relationship with God might be restored and renewed. God in Christ has done what we cannot do for ourselves. The Crucified One, who has been raised for the sake of all, now calls you beyond yourself and into a new and authentic way of living. Trust the promise and follow!

Presentation of Tithes and Offerings

What do we save by clinging to that which is not ours? What can we gain by such fruitless grasping? Shall we acquire the whole world at the cost of our souls? No. Rather, let us deny ourselves for the sake of Christ, who is generous and gracious and who fulfills God's promises to the faithful. We give to God in faith and trust.

Prayer of Dedication

Gracious God, we pay our vows to you with the great congregation, fulfilling our pledges as best we can, enacting with our giving that which we speak in our hearts. All honor and glory are due to you, for you feed the poor and can satisfy them, and you lift up those who go down to the dust. Turn our humble gesture into a mighty movement of your Spirit, part of the redeeming work of Jesus Christ our Lord.

The Blessing

Be not filled with the things of this world,
but take up your cross and follow in the Spirit.
Be not ashamed of the words of Jesus,
but make them your own and speak of Christ's glory.
Be not afraid of your losing your life,
but trust in the God who gave it to you,
who gives you a new one as you surrender the old.

Third Sunday in Lent

Exodus 20:1–17

Psalm 19

1 Corinthians 1:18–25

John 2:13–22

In Preparation for Worship

Crucified God,
with the foolishness of the cross, you save us;
with the weakness of your dying, we are made strong.
The wise of the world do not understand,
but we trust your ways
and worship you.

Call to Worship

Open your hearts and rejoice!
For the teaching of the Lord is right!
Open your eyes and see!
For the commandment of the Lord is clear!
Revive your souls and be free!
For the law of the Lord is good!
Be cleansed in heart, mind, soul, and body!
For the body is the temple of God.

Opening Prayer

Living God, you are ever present within us and without us. May we enter
your holy temple with hearts reverent toward your grace, minds open

to your wisdom, souls attuned to your holiness, for your glory and our sanctification.

CALL TO CONFESSION

The season for cleansing is upon us, the time for purifying the temple in which God dwells. For you yourselves are the Spirit's dwelling place. Will you not be zealous for God's sanctuary? Will you not welcome the healing of the Holy Spirit into your life? Will you not welcome the power of Christ into your spirit, soul, and body, directing God to the hurting places and allowing the Spirit to cut you loose from all ties to sin? Let us bear in mind the gift of the Ten Commandments as we confess our sins to God.

PRAYER OF CONFESSION

Holy God, we confess that we have wandered from your wisdom, which we have often regarded as folly. We have relied on our worldly wisdom, which, at its best, cannot compare even to your foolishness. For it is only by Christ's weakness, suffering, and death on the cross that we are saved. Forgive us, O God, and restore us to your grace, as we remember our humility before you and thank you for the marvelous gift of your Beloved Son for our salvation.

DECLARATION OF FORGIVENESS

By the commandments, we are duly warned, but in keeping them there is great reward! The same commandments that go out through all the earth, yet stand silent when we examine ourselves in their presence. In the silence we meet God's grace, we hear no voice of condemnation, we find we are free to begin again. Friends, seek the rewards that are found in obedience! Rejoice that you are free, and begin the Christian life anew!

PRESENTATION OF TITHES AND OFFERINGS

In turning over the tables of the money changers and pouring their coins out on the temple floor, Jesus cleansed the temple. But did he not also make an oblation, an offering of the money, setting sinners an example of how to consecrate their wealth? Let us offer up to God a similar outpouring. For in devoting our resources to God, they become the holy property of the holy God, and we are freed from bondage to them.

PRAYER OF DEDICATION

God of the Passover, we seek to be filled with zeal for your holy temple. As we lighten our earthly load of these treasures, purify them of their worldly appeal, sanctify them with the seal of the Spirit, so that in their use, justice may be served, righteousness may be done, suffering may be eased, and your glory may be increased forevermore.

THE BLESSING

Take the Holy Spirit into the temple of your body.
Take your place in the body of Christ.
Take God's gracious guidance deep into your hearts,
show it to the world, and seek the rewards of obedient faith.

Fourth Sunday in Lent

Numbers 21:4–9

Psalm 107:1–3, 17–22

Ephesians 2:1–10

John 3:14–21

In Preparation for Worship

Self-giving God, as we look to you, we are healed;
as we see you lifted up for our sake, we are humbled.
Hear our voices raised to your glory.
See our heads bowed before you.
Receive our hearts offered in trust
through your beloved and only begotten Son.

Call to Worship

We were once dead, under the rule of sin.
> **But God has made us alive again with Christ!**

We were once enslaved, bound by the desires of the flesh.
> **But the Spirit has stolen among us and set us free!**

We were once children of wrath, following the way of the world.
> **But we are raised with Christ by God's kindness!**

We are what God has made us, created in Christ for good works.
> **This is our way of life, which God prepared beforehand.**
> **Let us worship God!**

Opening Prayer

Gracious God, you are rich in mercy, saving us by grace through the faith of Jesus Christ, who is the perfect expression of your immeasurable goodness and your infinite love. We seek you, scarcely comprehending all that we owe you. Receive our thanks, our love, and our devotion.

Call to Confession

Those who cry out to the LORD in their distress, the LORD will surely save. God has sent the healing Holy Word, which is not only a spoken word of love and justice, but a Living Word, Jesus Christ. God claims those in trouble and gathers together all those whom Christ has called to forsake destructive lifestyles, and step forward for health, wholeness, and healing. God is greater than all our sins put together. Let us ask God, in confession, to rescue us from sin and all the consequences thereof.

Prayer of Confession

Almighty God, we confess that we have often run away from the light so that our sins might not be seen. We have remained in the sickness caused by our sin and drawn near to the gates of death. Send out your Word to heal us! Deliver us from death! Transform our darkness into the assurance of your eternal day, so that all our deeds may be done in the light and the love of your only Son, in whom we place our hope and trust.

Declaration of Forgiveness

The truth is this: God did not send Christ into the world to condemn the world but to save the world, and the price Jesus paid for you is staggering! Friends, if you trust in Christ Jesus you will be neither condemned nor judged; you will not die an eternal death, but will have life forevermore. Therefore, believe in Christ, live in the Spirit of truth, and enjoy the love of God!

Presentation of Tithes and Offerings

Grace, kindness, and immeasurable riches are ours in Christ Jesus! Therefore, we have plenty to spare, plenty to share! It is not by way of our goodness or generosity that it is so, but it comes to us as a gift from God to all who are raised from sin into lives of obedience. Let us share what we have from God.

Prayer of Dedication

Blessed God, you have given us life so that we might share in Christ's blessings. You have given us blessings so that, in sharing, we might also learn to let them go. We ask that your spirit of holiness would mark these gifts, so that they might be used in faith and that their use might bring you joy and honor and renown.

The Blessing

For good works you were created! Go and make your Maker proud!
In mercy you are saved from sin! Go and act with your Savior's mercy!
In truth you belong to the Spirit of Love!
Go and tell of God's great sacrifice of love!
For the blessings of Almighty God are alive and at work in you!

Fifth Sunday in Lent

Jeremiah 31:31–34
Psalm 51:1–12 OR Psalm 119:9–16
Hebrews 5:5–10
John 12:20–33

IN PREPARATION FOR WORSHIP

Almighty God,
let your voice thunder over us,
let the ruler of this world be driven out,
let your light so shine upon us
that we might be recognized
as your children of light!

CALL TO WORSHIP

Let the Messiah be exalted among us!
Let all the peoples of the earth draw near!
> The hour has come and we would see Jesus!
> The time has come to glorify the LORD!
Let those who would serve the Lord of life
follow Christ Jesus to the cross!
> Where the single seed falls, there is a full head of grain.
> Where our Lord has gone, let us faithfully follow.

OPENING PRAYER

Blessed One, we seek to know you and to know your ways. Help us to do so with our whole heart, to treasure your word in our inmost being, to receive a new and right spirit within us, that we might not forget your word, but delight to do your will in all things, through Jesus Christ our Lord.

Call to Confession

In the days of Jesus' fleshly and mortal body, he offered up prayers and supplications, with loud cries and tears, to the One who was able to save him from death, and he was heard because of his perfect submission. Although he was God's Son, Christ learned perfect obedience through suffering, and having been made perfect, became the source of eternal salvation for all who likewise obey. Therefore, let us lift up our cries, offer our tears, and surrender our grievances in obedience to Christ Jesus.

Prayer of Confession

O Jesus, our High Priest, you are the source of eternal salvation for all who obey you. We confess, however, that our obedience is wanting, our sin is great, and our need is profound. May your perfect sacrifice cover our sins, your steadfast faithfulness change our hearts, your Pure Spirit impart to us truth, obedience, and life, that we might serve you, praise you, please you, and know the deep, indwelling presence of God!

Declaration of Forgiveness

When the LORD washes us, we are truly clean. When Christ is lifted up on our behalf, the offering is perfect and complete. Receive with joy and gladness the good news of your salvation! Christ Jesus was sent into the world for this very purpose: to atone for the sins of the world!

Presentation of Tithes and Offerings

Should we not long for the day when there will be no more need to teach one another to know the LORD? Should we not work for the day when everyone, from the least to the greatest, will know the LORD? Let us dedicate our gifts to this great and happy goal, for this is what our covenant God desires! This is the salvific end for which God is working!

PRAYER OF DEDICATION

The offering we make, O Holy God, cannot be compared to the great sacrifice of Jesus Christ our Lord. Nevertheless, please accept these gifts as a sign of our obedience to you, a reminder of our mortality and accountability to you. Multiply each one for a plenteous, fruitful, and holy harvest. We ask this in Jesus' name.

THE BLESSING

The God whom Jesus called *Abba*, Father,
will honor those who serve the Christ.
Go, therefore, and serve your Savior,
obeying the Spirit, honorably and humbly,
and you will never be without
the presence of your LORD!

Sixth Sunday in Lent (*Palm Sunday*)

Isaiah 50:4–9a
Psalm 118:1–2, 19–29
Philippians 2:5–11
Mark 11:1–11 OR John 12:12–16

IN PREPARATION FOR WORSHIP

Hosanna, Lord, hosanna! We welcome you!
Set your face toward us, and come again for our salvation.
May we humble ourselves in your presence,
following your example of voluntary humility,
obedient even unto death.

CALL TO WORSHIP

Open the gates of righteousness!
Open the gates for our victorious Lord!
   Christ is our salvation!
   Hosanna! Hosanna!
Line the procession with branches!
Prepare the way for the anointed son of David!
   Christ is our cornerstone!
   Hosanna! Hosanna!
Give thanks to the LORD, for God is good!
   Christ is our mercy forever!
   Hosanna! Hosanna!

Opening Prayer

Blessed are you, Lord Jesus Christ! For you come to us, peaceful and lowly, riding on a donkey's colt. You come to give yourself for us. It is marvelous in our eyes! Therefore, we shall not be afraid.

Call to Confession

Do not be afraid or ashamed to bring your faults to the LORD. For God alone can give you the grace to grow into obedience and into the blessings that where his teachings are followed. God knows that we are vulnerable to sin and despair. This is why he sent Jesus to be our Lord and teacher, our friend and brother, as well as the atonement for our sins, and for the sins of all the world.

Prayer of Confession

Servant Lord, you call us to serve you and to serve one another. We confess that we are reluctant to stoop so low, yet when we do, we find you are already there, having taken the form of a slave. You have entered our lives not at the head of an army, but meekly, riding on a humble donkey. Teach us again your ways for living godly, compassionate lives of service. Forget our faults in your mercy, and make us anew in your image.

Declaration of Forgiveness

God has answered your prayers. Christ himself has become our salvation. The Lord is God, and has given us light to see with new eyes. God has opened our ears, awakening us morning by morning, to listen as those who are taught. It is the Lord who helps and saves you. Who then shall find you guilty?

Presentation of Tithes and Offerings

The offering of Jesus Christ was that he humbled himself and was wholly obedient, even to death on a cross. He did not exploit or take advantage of his privileged station as the Son of God, but shared humanity's pain and weakness so that we might share his perfected nature. Shall we withhold from such a Lord, or shall we give? Surely now is the time for us to give our best gifts to God.

Prayer of Dedication

Most gracious and generous God, let the measure of our gratitude be these gifts we offer you. Let your Holy Spirit forgive all that we cannot yet give. Let the name of your obedient One be praised and glorified. Let your reign come on earth by our reverent use of these, your blessed provisions.

The Blessing

Greet the Lord each morning with songs of praise. Claim the Lord each day as your Savior. Offer the Lord each night the day as you have lived it, and may all that you say, think, and do be a testimony to God's goodness, grace, and glory.

Seventh Sunday in Lent (*Passion Sunday*)

Isaiah 50:4–9a

Psalm 31:9–16

Philippians 2:5–11

Mark 14:1—15:47 OR Mark 15:1–39 (40–47)

IN PREPARATION FOR WORSHIP

O God our Deliverer, our times are in your hand!
Lift us up and let your face shine upon us,
that we might be awakened!

CALL TO WORSHIP

You who would have the mind of Christ,
come and worship the obedient One!
   Let every knee bow at the name of Jesus!
You who would learn from the Servant Teacher,
come and worship the self-emptying One!
   Let every tongue confess that Jesus is Lord!
You who would be saved from all manner of sin,
come and worship the innocent One!
   Jesus is Lord! Jesus is Lord!
   Christ Jesus makes known the glory of God!

OPENING PRAYER

O Christ our Redeemer, you did not speak in your own defense, you did
not hide your face from the blows, you did not flinch at the sting of the

scourge, you did not shrink from the cruelties of the cross! You, O Jesus, are our Suffering Savior! May your name be exalted forever!

CALL TO CONFESSION

Surely the LORD is near to the humble. For Christ Jesus, who is one with the Most High God, has taken the form of an obedient servant, that we might be saved through Christ's pure humanity and perfect sacrifice. It is the LORD who is our helper! Who then will declare us guilty, if we but confess our sin?

PRAYER OF CONFESSION

Gracious God, we call to you out of our distress! For there are forces that conspire against us, pains and sorrows that weigh upon us, accusing spirits that plot our downfall. We are all broken vessels, corrupted and unclean. We confess that we are too easily tempted and lured away from your purposes. We cannot repay the debt we owe you! Save us, O most merciful God, according to your steadfast love!

DECLARATION OF FORGIVENESS

The Lord Jesus Christ, when he hung upon the cross, was forsaken by God due to the sins of all the world with which he was laden. Our sins, which Jesus took upon himself, have died with him, and thus we are saved. As God's forgiven, we are the fruit of Christ's redeeming work, which God values most highly. For the sake of Jesus Christ, you are forgiven!

PRESENTATION OF TITHES AND OFFERINGS

God remembers us when the world forsakes us and delivers us when we are distressed. Should we not then have the mind of Christ, humble and obedient, toward the God who vindicates us? Should we exploit our equality with one another, or should we not rather take the form of servants toward one another? With this sharing of our gifts, let us testify to God's reign over all that we have and all that we are.

PRAYER OF DEDICATION

Because of your steadfast love, O LORD, we know that we can trust you to provide for us. Because of your deep compassion, we see in the Christ how you provide for our rescue from the eternal consequences of sin. Let nothing of this world come between us, O God, for we are yours, as are these gifts, to do with what you will.

The Blessing

Attend to the Spirit of the Lord as to a teacher.
Follow the Christ to the beckoning cross.
Trust in the one true God, your Creator,
that this saving word, this redeeming work,
is for you and for all those with whom
you share this good news.

Monday of Holy Week (ABC)

Isaiah 42:1–9

Psalm 36:5–11

Hebrews 9:11–15

John 12:1–11

In Preparation for Worship

Lamb of God,
you have given yourself to be anointed into death
so that we might join you in eternal life.
We exult in your gracious presence!
May our worship glorify you!

Call to Worship

Jesus Christ is the Lamb of God
who takes away the sin of the world.
> **Through the eternal Spirit, he offers himself.**
Jesus Christ is the Anointed, the High Priest.
> **Being without sin, he gives us a clean conscience.**
Jesus Christ is the Son of God,
the servant in whom God delights.
> **He purifies us of dead works,**
> **that we may worship the living God!**

Opening Prayer

You are the Lord! You alone give breath to your people, your Spirit to
those who walk in it. You have put your Spirit upon your Son, that he

might bring forth justice and righteousness. We bow to your gracious will! We welcome Christ's sovereign rule! For you alone are Lord!

Call to Confession

All people are invited to take refuge in the shadow of God's wings, to feast on the abundance of God's house, to drink from the river of delights. The steadfast love of the Lord is exceedingly precious, yet is available to all. For only in the light of God do we see things as they truly are! Therefore, draw near to the Lord in confession, that your eyes may be opened to God's unending love.

Prayer of Confession

O Holy Lord, when we are young, we often think we will live forever. As we grow older, enduring many losses, we recognize the reality of death. How is it that we can be at times so foolish, at other times so fearful? Have we taken you for granted, or have we not yet received you? Have we stopped trusting you, or have we not yet begun? Help us, Lord, to see your death for our sake as the precious gift that it is. Take our sin unto yourself on the cross, that it may be finally buried. Help us die to our persistent patterns of willful disobedience. Make us new and ever faithful, for your own name's sake.

Declaration of Forgiveness

Christ Jesus is the light to all the nations, a testimony to all people, upheld by God as the true witness to God's compassion, mercy, love, and justice! Let all who have sat in darkness emerge into the light of Christ, with whom we shall be raised, in whom we are truly forgiven.

Presentation of Tithes and Offerings

What costly thing will you offer to the One who withholds nothing from you, who is willingly emptied and poured out for you? What will you offer to the only One worthy to be the sacrifice, who did so willingly out of love for you? May your heart be full as you offer to the Lord your life, your love, your costly gift.

PRAYER OF DEDICATION

We thank you, O God, that you have given us a perfect priest of the good things to come! We thank you, Lord Jesus, that by your death, we are redeemed from transgressions under the old covenant. We thank you, Holy Spirit, that through you, the blood of Christ purifies our memories of dead works, that we may focus all our praise on the worship of the God of life! May our outpouring of these gifts be pleasing to you, and may they be a sign to the world of your abundant love and provision for all who long for your new creation.

THE BLESSING

Walk with the Spirit in compassion and justice!
Know that you share an inheritance with Christ!
Hold everything in the true light of God
and drink in the pure blessings from God's river of delights!

Tuesday of Holy Week (ABC)

Isaiah 49:1–7

Psalm 71:1–14

1 Corinthians 1:18–31

John 12:20–36

In Preparation for Worship

Lord, we have heard and now we heed your call.
We return to you, renouncing all that displeases you.
Help us now perform the true fast,
seeking your holiness above all else,
to your glory.

Call to Worship

The light is with you for a little longer.
Walk while you have the light
so that the darkness may not overtake you.
   Father, glorify your name!
Now is the judgment of this world.
Now the ruler of this world will be driven out.
   Father, glorify your name!
The hour has come for the Son of Man to be glorified.
Believe in the light while you have the light,
so that you may become children of light.
   Father, glorify your name!

Opening Prayer

O God, you are my rock and my fortress, my rescuer and my deliverer, my hope and my trust. Upon you I have leaned from my birth, for it was you who took me from my mother's womb. My mouth is filled with your praise and with your glory all day long. My praise is continually of you.

Call to Confession

God chooses what is foolish in the world to shame the wise. God chooses what is weak in the world to shame the strong. God chooses what is low and despised in the world, things that are not, to reduce to nothing things that are, so that no one might boast in the presence of God. God invites you, regardless of your station in life, to step forward and confess your foolishness, your weakness, your lowliness, your sin.

Prayer of Confession

Before you, O God, we surrender our wisdom, our knowledge, our discernment, our understanding. We lay down our pretentions, our pride, and our sin. For we stand in the presence of the crucified Christ who died to save the dying and those who believe. Bring us to faith, and our faith to fullness, you the Only Wise One, for surely our cause is with you!

Declaration of Forgiveness

He who died in weakness upon the cross has become for us wisdom from God, our righteousness, our sanctification, and our redemption. For as he said, "Unless a grain of wheat fall into the earth and dies, it remains but a single grain; but if it dies, it bears much fruit. . . . Those who love their life will lose it, and those who hate their life in this world, will keep it for eternity." Receive from Christ assurance of the forgiveness of sin. Do not neglect to leave the old life behind you, that it might die and you might bear much fruit.

Presentations of Tithes and Offerings

The reward of the servants of the LORD is with the LORD. You whom God has formed in the womb to be servants and raised up to be children of light, you who bear the name of Christ, consider how God has equipped you with the word of God as a sharp sword, with the light of God to shine in to the nations, with the saving power of the proclamation of Christ crucified: Consider and dedicate your lives, your gifts, and everything at your disposal to the service of Christ, for God the Father will honor whoever serves Jesus Christ the Son.

Prayer of Dedication

We whom you have chosen, O Gracious God, to enjoy so many blessings, have done nothing to deserve them. Therefore, we would ask your help, that we might share them with others whom you have also called, with those who may not yet know that they too are chosen and saved by you, our Gracious God. To this end we offer you these gifts.

The Blessing

Walk in the light of Christ crucified, who was crucified for you.
Trust in the light of the Spirit of Truth, the wisdom of God who teaches you.
Love the Light, the God of Glory, the Father of lights and Father to you,
for you are God's children, children of light!

Wednesday of Holy Week (ABC)

Isaiah 50:4–9a

Psalm 70

Hebrews 12:1–3

John 13:21–32

IN PREPARATION FOR WORSHIP

O LORD our God,
open our ears and make us steadfast in faith,
that we might not fall into rebellion or turn away
from Christ Jesus, your Son, the Obedient One.

CALL TO WORSHIP

Let all who seek the LORD rejoice!
Be glad in the LORD, for God is great!
> **Indeed, God is truly great!**
> **The LORD is our help and our deliverer.**
O LORD, make haste and do not delay!
For we are poor and needy.
> **Come quickly, O LORD, and hasten to help us!**
> **For we love your salvation, and we would praise you forevermore!**
May the LORD grant you an open ear and the gift of faith.
May your ears be awakened to listen as those who are taught.
> **Teach us, O LORD, and we will not turn back.**
> **Teach us to sustain the weary with your Word!**

Opening Prayer

Lord, draw near! Be near to us, for we would worship you! Be near to us, for we need you! Gather us anew into your holiness, that we might never stray from you or betray you. Surround us afresh with your great cloud of witnesses, that we might never forget all that you have done and all that you continue to do for us in Christ Jesus our Lord.

Call to Confession

Now is the time to lay aside every weight and the sin that clings so closely, to renounce every rebellious impulse—and to submit ourselves for examination to God, to ask for mercy and a clear conscience, in confident hope and expectation that the grace of the Lord is far greater than all human sin.

Prayer of Confession

God of Glory, hear our confession. We have received your gifts, but avoided responsibility; we have eaten your bread, but turned away from you; we have sought your blessings, but shunned the very sufferings by which you are glorified, by which we might glorify you. Therefore, let all fear and guilt, temptation and doubt, sin and evil depart from us, O Lord, for you alone are holy, and we would have you cleanse us, forgive us, and make us holy, through the gracious perfection of your Son, Jesus Christ our Lord.

Declaration of Forgiveness

Surely God is your helper. Who then shall declare you guilty? The Lord has vindicated you. Who, then, shall contend with you? God is near! Therefore, set your face toward the goal and run with perseverance the race that is set before you, "looking to Jesus, the pioneer and perfecter of our faith, who for the sake of the joy that was set before him, endured the cross, and disregarding its shame, has taken his seat at the right hand of the throne of God." For it is in Christ and through his atoning work that you are forgiven.

PRESENTATION OF TITHES AND OFFERINGS

Let gifts be given with a pure heart, with faithful devotion, with a joyful and generous spirit! Let us commit our gifts to the will, the purpose, the mission of our God, from whom comes every good and perfect gift.

PRAYER OF DEDICATION

O most generous God, our Father, you who did not withhold your only Son Jesus Christ, but who gave him up for our vindication; you who sustain us from day to day, with a fresh word for our weary souls—guide and direct us in the good and fruitful use of these tithes and offerings, that those who do not yet know you might receive and believe the good news of the forgiveness of sins and eternal life in Christ, and that those of us who do know you in part, might receive sustenance for faith and hope and love in this life, until we know you fully in eternity.

THE BLESSING

Seek the joy that is set before you!
Persevere in faith, come what may!
Look to Jesus, both seated on high with his eye upon you,
and near to you to help, deliver, and sustain you in all things.

Maundy Thursday (ABC)

Exodus 12:1–4 (5–10) 11–14

Psalm 116:1–2, 12–19

1 Corinthians 11:23–26

John 13:1–17, 31b–35

IN PREPARATION FOR WORSHIP

Gracious Lord,
we come to remember your marvelous life
and your passion for our salvation.
May your Spirit of humble service possess our congregation.
May your Spirit of Love fill our worship, to your glory.

CALL TO WORSHIP

What shall we give unto God for all God has given for us?
We lift up the cup of salvation
and call on the name of the LORD!
What shall we say unto God who so values all our lives?
We offer our thanks and praise
and call on the name of the LORD!
What shall we do in service to God, who hears all our prayers?
We pay our vows in the presence of God's people
and call upon the name of the LORD!

OPENING PRAYER

God of the exodus, by the flesh of the Passover Lamb, you feed us for the
journey; by the blood of the Passover Lamb, you exempt us from death's

finality. We praise you that by sending Jesus to be the Holy Lamb, once and for all, you have made possible the journey through death and into eternal life. May your holy name, and that of your holy Son, be praised forever!

Call to Confession

It is in remembering that we are unworthy of God's gift of Christ Jesus that we are made worthy. It is in finding our Lord washing our feet that we recognize the grace, love, and tenderness with which God cares for us. Be not afraid to confess your sin to such a God as this!

Prayer of Confession

Gracious God, we have been baptized, but our feet are dusty from the road, tired from the journey. Though you have bathed us in your Spirit and in the blood of your Son, yet we continue to participate in the sin of this world. Cleanse us again from head to toe. Renew us for lives of earthly discipleship and heavenly service.

Declaration of Forgiveness

The Lord has set us an example of how we are to serve one another. Just as he has washed our feet and forgiven us for our stumbling, so we too must wash one another's feet and forgive each other. This is life under the government of grace: that we should forgive one another graciously, just as we have been forgiven.

Presentation of Tithes and Offerings

What shall we return to God for all the bounty we have received? Thank offerings, vows of faith, lives lived in love, praise, joy, and obedience to our God. Let us glorify God with our gifts!

Prayer of Dedication

As you, O Christ, have given your body for us, we dedicate our bodily life to you. As you, O Christ, have given your living blood for us, we dedicate our living to you. May these resources, given in deep and reverent gratitude, take on new life in your service. May we, the givers, reflect something of your grand generosity in giving your body and blood, indeed your very earthly life, for us!

THE BLESSING

Take up your staff! The LORD calls you to leave every form of slavery!
Begin the journey! You have been fed by Jesus Christ, the Paschal Lamb!
Call upon the Spirit of God with every breath given you,
giving thanks to Christ Jesus in all that you do!

Good Friday (ABC)

Isaiah 52:12—53:12

Psalm 22

Hebrews 10:16–25 OR Hebrews 4:14–16; 5:7–9

John 18:1—19:42

IN PREPARATION FOR WORSHIP

Suffering God, by your wounds we are healed,
by your blood we are cleansed,
by your Spirit we are made one with you in your death and in your life.
As you have died, may all our sins, and death itself, die with you.

CALL TO WORSHIP

Enter with confidence the sanctuary of our God!
For Christ has opened for us a new and living way!
We enter only by the blood of Jesus,
through his own flesh which he has offered up!
Such is the faithfulness of our great high priest, Jesus Christ,
who embodies the full assurance of our faith!
We enter into a new covenant with the LORD,
cherishing the laws of God in our hearts,
finding our consciences sprinkled clean and our bodies washed
by pure water and the blood of Christ. Praise be to God!

OPENING PRAYER

Loving God, you have shown us the depths of your love by experiencing
the depths of human pain for us and by patiently enduring the world's

rejection. How can we ever thank you enough or aspire to love as you have loved?

CALL TO CONFESSION

When the life of the Messiah becomes an offering for the sin in your life, Christ acknowledges you as a true child of God. Through the Righteous One, Jesus, the Suffering Servant of God, the will of God shall prosper, and God's will is that you should be healed by Christ's wounds, that Christ should bear the punishment that makes every sinner whole again. Let us all confess our deep need of forgiveness and consider our Lord's awesome gift.

PRAYER OF CONFESSION

Holy God, what are we to say in your presence? Christ is perfect. We are imperfect. Christ is sinless. We have sinned. Christ has received the full payment for the sins of the world. Forgive us, Lord, as we rend our hearts before you, as we open our lives to you, as we seek anew to live in gratitude for the unspeakable grace of your righteous Servant and our Savior, in whose name we pray.

DECLARATION OF FORGIVENESS

Jesus Christ has become the source of eternal salvation for all who obey him! Therefore, let us consider how to provoke one another to love and good deeds, to joyful fellowship and mutual encouragement, so that we might stand with bold confidence on the fast approaching Day of the Lord.

PRESENTATION OF TITHES AND OFFERINGS

Jesus has become our pattern for humble obedience and reverent submission. One way in which we can practice conforming our lives to his pattern is by acts of self-giving and surrender. Surely no material gift can compare with the suffering of our Lord, who offered up prayers and supplications, loud cries and tears, as he died upon the cross. But with our humble offerings, we can testify to where our true affections lie: not with the things of this world, but with our Savior, Jesus Christ, our great high priest who has passed through the heavens.

PRAYER OF DEDICATION

You are holy, O God, forever enthroned upon the praises of your people, and holy is your Son, the Sinless One, who has opened for us the new and living way to you! May these offerings of our gratitude be a witness to those of future generations, inspired, confirmed, and sealed in your Holy Spirit, that you are most worthy, righteous, and compassionate, and that you, our Deliverer, have done it!

THE BLESSING

Consider the price that Jesus Christ has paid for you,
and aspire to live a life in keeping with that infinite value.
Consider the eternal benefits of this holy atonement and reconciliation,
and breathe anew in the Holy Spirit of freedom.
Consider the love of God in this: that you have been chosen to enter
by way of grace, with Christ, into his most holy presence,
where you will forever be at home with God!

Easter (*The Resurrection of the Lord*)

Acts 10:34–43 OR Isaiah 25:6–9
Psalm 118:1–2,14–24
1 Corinthians 15:1–11 OR Acts 10:34–43
John 20:1–18 OR Mark 16:1–8

IN PREPARATION FOR WORSHIP

Lord God of Hosts,
you have prepared a feast
of rich food and pure fruit of the vine.
Come eat with us again, as you did with your disciples,
that we may be witnesses of your resurrection,
telling the good news to all the world.

CALL TO WORSHIP

Death is swallowed up forever!
Alleluia! Let us be glad and rejoice!
Let every tear be wiped away!
Alleluia! Let us be glad and rejoice!
Jesus Christ is our salvation, and He is risen from the dead!
This is our God: the Risen Son!
We have waited for the LORD,
and Christ Jesus has saved us! Alleluia! Amen!

OPENING PRAYER

Holy, Risen Lord, you have taken on sin and death and you have defeated
them. You have rolled the stone away from the tomb, leaving it powerless

and void. In awe and wonder we praise you, amazed at the new reality of your Easter morning. May this newness change the way we see the world, so that we may no longer fear death, but cherish both this life and the life to come as precious gifts from your loving hand.

Call to Confession

Christ has died, but he has overcome death. Christ both reigns on high and lives again in you and me, that we might display God's wondrous deeds. So bring your sins and sorrows to the One whom death has not defeated. Christ alone has the power to grant your desire for healing and holy living. Let us confess God's righteousness and our sin.

Prayer of Confession

God of the empty tomb, you have not abandoned your Son, neither have you allowed his body to experience corruption and decay, but your Holy Spirit has raised him from the dead. Yet we, his body, fail and falter when it comes to trusting the good news and performing your perfect will. Lift us out of our fears and worries. Heal us by his holy wounds. Guide us back out onto the road with the message that you are the eternal God: suffering, forgiving, risen, and gracious.

Declaration of Forgiveness

Jesus himself was sent by God to preach peace, to be raised in glory from death, to judge the living and the dead. His peace is available to all people in every land and nation, for God shows no partiality. All the prophets testify about Jesus that everyone who believes in him receives forgiveness of sins through his name. Beloved friends, fear the LORD! Do what is right! Believe in Jesus Christ, and know that you are forgiven.

Presentation of Tithes and Offerings

Let us give thanks to the LORD, for God is good; the steadfast love and mercy of the LORD endure forever! How might our acts of thanksgiving take on such endurance and eternal significance? Only by participating in what God is doing through his chosen, forgiven people! Let us give our gifts to God, so that we might participate in God's plan for Christ's coming kingdom.

PRAYER OF DEDICATION

Risen Lord, you have become our salvation. Your rejection by others has bought us a sure foundation. Build with these gifts upon your cornerstone. Create with these tools another of your mighty works, marvelous in our eyes. We offer them with songs of praise, shouts of joy, and hymns of thanksgiving, in Jesus' name.

THE BLESSING

The Scriptures are fulfilled! The tomb is empty!
The grave clothes are cast aside!
Step out into the new creation! Go and tell this generation!
Go and tell the world: Jesus Christ is Lord, and he has risen from the dead!

Easter Evening (ABC)

Isaiah 25:6–9

Psalm 114

1 Corinthians 5:6b–8

Luke 24:13–49

IN PREPARATION FOR WORSHIP

LORD, you have shaken our reality.
The mountains and hills are no longer sure,
the rivers and seas no longer reliable,
and death itself no longer final.
LORD, you have shaken our reality with joy!
We are so glad that we have waited for you!

CALL TO WORSHIP

Tremble, O earth, at the presence of the LORD!
The mountains and hills, the sea and the land,
tremble and flee at the presence of our long-awaited LORD.
Be glad and rejoice at the salvation of the LORD!
The LORD has wiped our tears away.
Death is swallowed up forever!
Rejoice and give thanks in the presence of our risen Lord!
The Lord is risen indeed!
Alleluia! Amen!

Opening Prayer

Giver of life and of eternal life, we come to the end of this Easter day, rapt in wonder, alive in hope. As Cleopas and the other disciple received bread from the hands of the risen Jesus, we too would keep the feast with you, would celebrate new life with you, for you are gracious to allow each of us to share in your resurrection life.

Call to Confession

Let no one retain the old, worthless ways of malice, evil, pride, or boastfulness. But let us confess our sin to God our deliverer, and ask that we be formed afresh, in purity, sincerity, and truth.

Prayer of Confession

God of the Resurrection, we confess that we are foolish, fearful, doubtful, forgetful. We live most of our lives heedless of your presence with us. We allow doubts to arise in our hearts and to cloud our understanding. We allow fears to paralyze us as we wonder how to respond to your sheer, glorious goodness. Forgive us, LORD, for our foolish ways. Speak peace to our troubled hearts. Lead us in the everlasting way.

Declaration of Forgiveness

You are God's witnesses in this generation! Therefore, familiarize yourselves with the law, the prophets, the psalms, and the many promises fulfilled in Christ Jesus. Proclaim repentance and the forgiveness of sins that you yourselves have received through the suffering of your once dead and now risen Savior! This news is too good not to share!

Presentation of Tithes and Offerings

With such simple elements as bread and fish, our risen Savior reminds us that the blessed word of the LORD is to be multiplied and shared and spread abroad. Therefore, give testimony with the elements that God has entrusted to you, that Christ Jesus is risen in accordance with the Scriptures. Show forth the good news gladly in the sharing of your gifts.

Prayer of Dedication

O God our Consolation, who tasted death for all and gives life to all, we anticipate the rich feast which you are preparing for all people on your holy mountain. Receive and bless these our humble contributions, that they might enable others to discover the joy of knowing you and celebrating with you in this life and at the eternal, heavenly banquet that you are preparing for all peoples, O God our blessed Consolation.

The Blessing

May the Holy Spirit enliven you and quicken your hearts.
May the risen Christ empower you and instruct your minds.
May the Lord of hosts startle you with delight and wonder and joy.
For the creating, saving, and re-creating God is with you on your journey!
Go in peace and proclaim the good news!
Christ Jesus is risen! He is the Lord of life! He is the Lord of new life!

Second Sunday of Easter

Acts 4:32–35
Psalm 133
1 John 1:1—2:2
John 20:19–31

In Preparation for Worship

Holy Three in One,
you are of one Heart, Mind, and Holy Spirit.
Make us one with our risen Lord and with each other
as you raise us into new hope, new faith, new life,
in Jesus' name.

Call to Worship

God of Glory, you are light!
In you, O God, there is no darkness!
Son of Light, you are truth!
In you, O Christ, there is no falsehood!
Spirit of Truth, you are righteous!
In you, O Spirit, there is no sin!
Atoning Lord, we praise your holy name!
**For by all your names and words and deeds,
you alone are holy!**

Opening Prayer

Eternal God, you have not only raised Jesus Christ from the dead, you have graciously allowed your Son to reveal himself risen. This witness has come down to us through the ages. We thank you. Breathe upon us, once again, your vital Holy Spirit, that we, as your chosen disciples, may be inspired to take up the holy tasks of discerning and forgiving, of teaching and sharing, of witnessing and caring, making the best use of the time you have given us.

CALL TO CONFESSION

All who have the truth within them admit their need for the grace of God. All who deny their need for grace, lie and make God into a liar. Let us all be truthful this day and confess our sins to God. For God is always faithful, even when we have not been. God is always just and fair, even though we are not. In the blood of Jesus Christ, God has anticipated our need for forgiveness, and given us the means to receive it.

PRAYER OF CONFESSION

God of the Resurrection, we confess to you that we do not trust what we cannot see. Like Thomas, we prefer to see with our eyes, and only then believe in our hearts. Where we lack trust in the certainty of the life to come, forgive us, and increase our faith. Where we live as if this life on earth is our last chance at happiness, have mercy on us, and sharpen our vision. Where we continue to sin and fall short of your glory, erase our mistakes by the grace of Jesus Christ, and give us resolve to live in the light of his presence with us.

DECLARATION OF FORGIVENESS

The risen Lord first greeted those who had deserted him by saying, "Peace be unto you!" And again he said, "Peace be unto you!" He then gave to those whom he had forgiven the authority to forgive. They did not go to him asking to be forgiven. He came upon them, behind their doors locked in fear, and showed his wounds, and shared his peace, and gave to them of his Spirit. Such is Christ's determination to forgive. Friends in Christ, trust in our risen Lord and Advocate. Know that you are forgiven.

PRESENTATION OF TITHES AND OFFERINGS

The Scriptures testify to the fact that those in the early church shared everything in common, and not one of them had any need. With one heart and soul, let us share what we have with God and God's people so that grace will be upon us all.

PRAYER OF DEDICATION

Gracious God, as we have received, so help us to give; as any have need, so direct us to share; as Christ is risen, so raise the level of our being, beyond concern for worldly wealth, to participate in the joy of your heavenly kingdom.

THE BLESSING

May the Spirit of God be stirred within you.
May the heart of Christ bid love to reign.
May the hand of God bestow grace upon you
and guide you along the narrow way.

Third Sunday of Easter

Acts 3:12–19

Psalm 4

1 John 3:1–7

Luke 24:36b–48

In Preparation for Worship

Risen Redeemer God,
in your revealed presence
is our future and our salvation.
We seek your glory. We seek your face.

Call to Worship

Answer me when I call, O God!
You gave me room when I was in distress.
   Let the light of your face shine upon us, O Lord!
How long, you people, will God's honor suffer shame?
How long will you love vain words, and seek after lies?
   Let the light of your face shine upon us, O Lord!
When you are disturbed, do not sin;
but ponder it on your beds, and be silent!
Offer right sacrifices, and put your trust in the Lord!
   Let the light of your face shine upon us, O Lord!
I will both lie down and sleep in peace;
for you alone, O Lord, make me lie down in safety.
   Let the light of your face shine upon us, O Lord!

Opening Prayer

Holy and Righteous God, your holy name heals and strengthens us. May we find faith to trust in you entirely, even as children instinctively trust a loving father. May we hope in you always, and thus be made pure, holy, and perfect in your likeness.

Call to Confession

All who have hope in Jesus Christ are purified by this hope. In Christ, there is no sin, and when he is revealed to us and we receive him, he takes away our sins. Therefore, arise out of your despair and doubt. Go ahead and get your hopes up! Bring them to Christ in confession, so that he may reveal himself to you as the healer of your wounds, the forgiver and forgetter of all your sins.

Prayer of Confession

O God our Creator, your risen Son has made it possible for us to be your children. Yet we confess we have continued in sin and lawlessness, refusing to hope, ignoring the immediacy of your real presence with us, postponing giving you your due authority over our lives. Re-create us, God, for faith, for hope, for acts of love and compassion, that we might conform to the glorious image of your gracious and merciful Son.

Declaration of Forgiveness

Let repentance and forgiveness of sins be proclaimed to all nations in the name of Jesus Christ. Let your sins be wiped out! For this very reason, God has fulfilled all that was written about the Messiah by the prophets from the time of Moses, and in the Psalms. God has been planning your salvation through Christ from the beginning. Believe in the power of the name of Jesus Christ and receive the gift of eternal life.

Presentation of Tithes and Offerings

When God puts gladness in our hearts, it is better than the finest feast or the brightest day. As God sets apart those who are faithful, let us set apart a portion of our many blessings to enact and demonstrate our faith. Let us offer right sacrifices, and put our trust in the Lord.

PRAYER OF DEDICATION

The greatest blessing we have, O God, is to be called your children. What can we offer you to compare with such a gift? Receive these tokens as our act of faith and love, and in our giving, make us more like you.

THE BLESSING

God is our loving Father. Therefore, love your God!
Christ is revealed to take away all sin. Therefore, live in Christ!
The Spirit is in you to inspire holy living. Therefore, listen to the Spirit!
And the light of God, Creator, Christ, and Holy Spirit,
shine upon you and give you peace!

Fourth Sunday of Easter

Acts 4:5–12

Psalm 23

1 John 3:16–24

John 10:11–18

In Preparation for Worship

Jesus Christ, crucified and risen,
you saved your apostles from sin and prison;
fulfill us now with purpose and vision
as we seek to worship you.

Call to Worship

The Good Shepherd lays down his life for his sheep.
> **Let us love, not in word or speech alone,**
> **but in truth and action.**

The Good Shepherd leads us, and restores our souls.
> **Let us love one another**
> **as Christ has commanded us.**

The Good Shepherd is our Lord and God!
> **We shall not want; therefore,**
> **let us lay down our lives for one another.**

Opening Prayer

Holy Lord, you are the one true Shepherd and we are the sheep of your
pasture. We await the sound of your familiar voice. Speak to us. Lead us.

Show us the way through your paths of righteousness, toward greener pastures, by your still, living waters, to our eternal home with you.

Call to Confession

As the apostles said when they were filled with the Holy Spirit: "There is salvation in no one other than Jesus Christ, for there is no other name under heaven by which we may be saved." Just as the apostles healed in the name of Jesus, so we too have hope of healing and forgiveness by his very name. Let us confess our sins, and ask for and receive a fresh start in the name of the one who alone can grant it.

Prayer of Confession

All-knowing God, we say that we love you, yet we confess that our lives all too rarely show it. We say that your love is alive within us, yet we all too often let the needs of others go unmet. How can we say that we love you when we do not obey your commandment to love one another? Yet you, O Lord, are greater than any falsity in our hearts! Forgive us, and increase your love within us, that we may truly host your indwelling Holy Spirit, love one another as Christ has loved us, and live to your praise and glory, in Jesus' name.

Declaration of Forgiveness

We know by this that we are loved: that Jesus Christ was willing to lay down his life for us. Let us receive God's forgiveness, even as we receive Christ's love. God's great commandment is to love one another, just as Christ has loved us. And the promise of loving is this: that we may be bold before God and receive whatever we ask because of our obedience to this rule of love. Friends, make that fresh start. You are forgiven in Christ. Now love one another in Christ.

Presentation of Tithes and Offerings

One way we demonstrate and enact our love for God is by sharing openly with one another and with those in especial need. If God's love abides in us, we will be not only caring, but also sharing people. Let us give to God, through Christ's holy Church, with generosity, commitment, and love.

PRAYER OF DEDICATION

O God, who makes our cups overflow, receive these outpourings of our love for you and bless them with your holiness, that we might, through your Church, care for one another, for this community of faith, and for your world.

THE BLESSING

Trust the LORD to lead and to feed you;
trust in Christ to save and forgive you;
trust the Holy Spirit to strengthen and empower you,
and ask—and receive whatever you ask—in love.

Fifth Sunday of Easter

Acts 8:26–40

Psalm 22:25–31

1 John 4:7–21

John 15:1–8

IN PREPARATION FOR WORSHIP

Holy Vinegrower,
we come to you,
hoping to bear much fruit for your glory.
Cleanse us with your Living Word,
stimulate our growth,
and fill us with your Holy Spirit.

CALL TO WORSHIP

Apart from Christ, we can do nothing.
Let us seek to live in Christ,
as the branches have life from the vine.
Apart from God, we cannot bear fruit.
Let us seek God's glory
as we bear good fruit for the vinegrower.
Apart from the Spirit, we cannot love.
Let us seek to love,
because God has first loved us.

OPENING PRAYER

Living, loving God, you are love, and we long to be like you. When we love
we have the assurance of knowing that you are alive within us, and that

your love is perfected in us. Now stir up your life and your love within, among, and between us, that as we seek to serve you, we might worship you in truth and in love, in Jesus' name. Amen.

CALL TO CONFESSION

"All the ends of the earth shall remember and turn to the LORD." Now is the time for such remembering, for turning our hearts to God. We remember that we are dust, that we will all go down to the dust, even as we remember and rejoice that God can make the dust to live again. We turn away from sin and turn to God, remembering and trusting that all who seek the LORD shall live to praise the LORD! Let us confess our sin.

PRAYER OF CONFESSION

Creator God, you love us so deeply that you have given Jesus Christ, your only begotten Son, to be the atoning sacrifice for our sins. Yet, we confess that we have not consistently considered ourselves dead to sin; we have not always answered your love with love; we have not always responded to your voice calling us to obedience; we have not always shared the love of Christ with others. Forgive us. Prune and cleanse us. Free us from sin and liberate us for loving, in Jesus' name.

DECLARATION OF FORGIVENESS

The gardener God does not cast off those branches that dwell in Christ, the true vine. Indeed, it is in our remaining connected to Christ that we have our life, our fruitfulness, and our forgiveness. Those who remain in Christ shall live, and have nothing to fear. Therefore, be at peace. In Jesus Christ, you are forgiven.

PRESENTATION OF TITHES AND OFFERINGS

God has not only given Jesus Christ to atone for our sins and to give us life. God has also given us the Holy Spirit to live with us and in us, so that we might live with God in love. Such a self-giving God deserves all that we are willing to give and much more. So offer your best to God in love and thankfulness.

Prayer of Dedication

Bountiful God, we wish to share with you all that you have shared with us. You have imparted your Holy Spirit to us. Therefore, in your Spirit, we lift up this collection to you in love and in an attitude of humble service, asking for your divine blessing, that we might use it to tell the world of your goodness to us in Jesus Christ.

The Blessing

Live in love, and the Spirit of Life will fill you with good things.
Live in truth, and the True Vine will keep you alive in Christ.
Live in God, and all the blessings that you ask of God will be given.

Sixth Sunday of Easter

Acts 10:44–48

Psalm 98

1 John 5:1–6

John 15:9–17

In Preparation for Worship

Let the clapping flood and the roaring sea,
the rising hills and the whole earth,
all nations, all peoples, the righteous, and me,
laud you, O Lord, and sing of your worth!

Call to Worship

Our love of God is evident in this, that we obey the commandments of God.
> **We have not chosen God, but God has chosen us!**
> **Therefore, let us love one another as Christ has loved us!**
The victory that conquers the world is faith!
> **What does it mean to conquer the world?**
> **We do so in believing that Jesus is the Christ!**
The One to whom the Spirit testifies is Christ Jesus.
> **As the Spirit is the truth, so Christ is also the truth!**
> **Let us worship the Lord God in spirit and in truth!**

Opening Prayer

Loving God, who has sent forth the Christ with water and blood, who
dispenses the Spirit in abundance, we thank you that we may rely on you
to be the truth, we bless you that we may abide in you for the sake of love,

we praise you that we may reside in you with complete joy! May the joyful sounds we make this day give you joy and honor and pleasure!

CALL TO CONFESSION

The LORD is coming to judge the earth, to judge the world with righteousness and the peoples with equity! God will come looking for love, for the fruits of love borne in accordance with the commandment of Christ that we should love one another. Those who love have nothing to fear. Therefore, let us confess our sin, remembering that Jesus has expressed the greatest love for us, in laying down his life for us in order to do away with our sins and all their wretched consequences.

PRAYER OF CONFESSION

Gracious God, through Jesus Christ you have made known to us that which you have appointed us to do. Are we yielding the fruit that will last, or are we dying upon the vine? Do we lovingly obey you as friends of Christ Jesus your Son, or are we separating ourselves from your holy purposes? Hear our honest admission, O God, that we need you, that we can do nothing apart from you, that we wish to remain in you and to learn to live in your love!

DECLARATION OF FORGIVENESS

Christ has not only saved you, but he has chosen you to bear lasting fruit. Christ has not only given up his life for you, but he has called you to be his friends. Christ has not only commanded you to love, but he places his holy joy within you so that your joy may be complete. These are the measures to which the Lord Jesus is willing to go for you. Therefore, be assured of God's love and mercy toward you, and be at peace.

PRESENTATION OF TITHES AND OFFERINGS

Shall we praise God with songs and words only, or shall we allow the Holy Spirit to move us to works of love and acts of faith? Whatever is born of God conquers the world! Therefore, let the love of God bring forth generous deeds among you, that we might have victory over the world through faith!

PRAYER OF DEDICATION

Lord Jesus, you are the Christ, the Son of the Living God! We declare it with our testimony, and we would proclaim it by devoted giving and obedient living! Guide us in our using and sharing of these gifts, that in our doing so, the world might witness your love at work in us, confirmed and empowered by the Spirit of truth!

THE BLESSING

Abide in the love of Christ Jesus, your Risen Lord!
Seek the Holy Spirit with the truth of God's Word!
Love God, who is coming to judge the world!
May the love of the LORD be seen among you,
and soon your joy will be made complete!

Ascension of the Lord (ABC)

Acts 1:1–11

Psalm 47 OR **Psalm 93**

Ephesians 1:15–23

Luke 24:44–53

IN PREPARATION FOR WORSHIP

Crucified Lord, you arise!
Risen Lord, you ascend!
Ascended Lord, you reign over all!
Fill all those who gather to give you glory,
that we might worship you in the spirit of wisdom.

CALL TO WORSHIP

God has gone up with a shout!
> **Let us sing loud songs of joy!**
> **Sing praises to God!**

Christ has been carried up to heaven!
> **Let us sound the trumpet!**
> **Bless God in the holy temple!**

Come, Holy Spirit!
> **Come, Lord Jesus! Just as you ascended in the cloud,**
> **come again to receive your holy people!**

OPENING PRAYER

Steadfast God, you keep your covenant in spite of our sin. You keep promises, even in the face of death. You keep the outcast close by you, and lift up your rejected Son to rule at your side. May we learn and grow to be as faithful as Christ was obedient, as loyal as the Spirit is true, as holy as your love that fills your whole creation!

CALL TO CONFESSION

Before he ascended into heaven, Jesus charged the disciples to preach repentance and forgiveness of sins to all nations. The message is for everyone, but one does not happen without the other. Forgiveness hinges on our change of heart, just as repentance becomes our greatest desire only when we realize the depth of God's patience with us, and God's eagerness to give us a new life in Christ. Let us confess our sin, truly repenting of the pain that we have caused God and one another.

PRAYER OF CONFESSION

O Lord Most High, you set the times and seasons for everything. Yet we must confess how impatient we are. We long for answers that are yours alone to know, and lose sight of the joy of simply being with you while we live. Calm our troubled hearts, which cause us to sin. Steady our spirits with your powerful peace. Forgive our sullied souls, and breathe new life into us with your Holy Spirit.

DECLARATION OF FORGIVENESS

God calls us to hope, and does not do so without purpose. God uses the greatness of the power of the Holy Spirit on our behalf, putting this power to work in Jesus Christ by raising him from the dead and seating our gracious Lord at the right hand of power in heaven. All this God has done and continues to do for us, not against us, so that we might have hope of life without sin.

PRESENTATION OF TITHES AND OFFERINGS

Having promised the coming of the Holy Spirit, Jesus was taken up into heaven. Yet, even as he was being taken up, he blessed his disciples. Such is the constancy and continuity with which we are blessed by God. Let us therefore imitate our God by giving continually, regularly, faithfully, consistently.

Prayer of Dedication

Almighty God, who has raised Christ from death to new life, and from new life to power on high, we praise you with these gifts for your life-giving Spirit. We thank you with these blessings for having so richly blessed us. We know that our glorious inheritance is with you, and that there is nothing of this earth more precious than knowing and serving our Savior and Lord, Jesus Christ, in whose name we dedicate this offering.

The Blessing

Take this news into your hearts: the Son of God, who was dead, now reigns.
Take this news into your souls: the Spirit is coming. Wait for it!
Take this news into the world: the Creator is Lord over all creation.
Live your life in subjection and in service to the three-in-one God.

Seventh Sunday of Easter

Acts 1:15–17, 21–26
Psalm 1
1 John 5:9–13
John 17:6–19

IN PREPARATION FOR WORSHIP

Watchful God,
we come to meditate upon your word,
to plant ourselves in your holy presence
like trees beside streams of living water.
May we give you glory as you make us prosper.

CALL TO WORSHIP

The LORD knows all our hearts.
Let us welcome Christ into our lives.
The Spirit has testified concerning the holy name of Jesus Christ.
Let us receive the testimony of the Spirit.
The Father gives us eternal life, and this life is in his Son.
Let us begin eternal life today, for the one who has the Son of God has eternal life in him.

OPENING PRAYER

Eternal God, who makes the righteous to prosper and the wicked to fall away, count us among your righteous, set us apart for goodness, make us wholly obedient to the truth, so that as we declare your holiness to the world, we might be one with you and with your Son, Jesus Christ, in whose name we pray.

Call to Confession

Christ himself prayed for his disciples, not that God should take them out of the world, but that they would be protected from the evil one. The purpose of this prayer, according to his very own words, was so that his followers might have his very own joy made complete in themselves. If you are frustrated or fed up with sin; if you are bruised and broken by the violence and corruption of this world; if you are discouraged or disappointed with any part or all of your life, confess it to God now and learn this: Jesus Christ has something much more pure, much more joyful in mind for you, indeed, for all of us. Let us confess our sin to God.

Prayer of Confession

Righteous God, there are two ways through this world. We confess that we have not remained faithful to the righteous way. We do not meditate upon your law as we should, nor have we sought to delight in it. Forgive us, God. Block every path that leads to destruction. Steer us into healthy, hopeful ways, that we might know your joy completely, to the glory of our gracious Lord Jesus.

Declaration of Forgiveness

No matter what anyone says, what God says is greater: that eternal life is yours if you accept the life given to you in Christ. There is no condemnation for those who live in Christ, but an invitation to holy living and complete joy!

Presentation of Tithes and Offerings

The Lord knows everyone's heart, seeing everything that is hidden there. Indeed, nothing can be hidden and no one can hide from the Lord. Thus the apostles and saints offered their whole lives to God to be witnesses to the resurrection. Let us do likewise.

Prayer of Dedication

As you have given us your word, O God, so we respond in faith. If we belong to you, O Lord, then so do all our most precious gifts. Sanctify us in truth, and with us, all that you have given us, so that your truth might be known in us, and shown to the world through us.

The Blessing

You no longer belong to the world, but you belong to the Word of God. Take this holy Word, the Spirit of Christ, and walk in the righteous ways of God.

Pentecost

Acts 2:1–21 OR Ezekiel 37:1–14

Psalm 104:24–34, 35b

Romans 8:22–27 OR Acts 2:1–2

John 15:26–27; 16:4b–15

IN PREPARATION FOR WORSHIP

O Holy Helper, Paraclete,
Spirit of Truth, our Advocate:
Come with wisdom from on high!
Come in truth and testify!
We watch, we wait, we hope, we sigh!
O search our hearts and purify!

CALL TO WORSHIP

Let God's people of faith be gathered together.
Let the devout wait for the outpouring of the LORD!
    Send your Holy Spirit upon us.
    Fill this place with your heavenly wind!
Let each heart be open to welcome the Holy Spirit.
Let each one receive the blessed gift of God!
    Send your Holy Spirit upon us!
    Light each one with your living tongues of flame!
Let your eyes be opened to the revelation of God.
Let your mouths be filled with the word of the LORD!
    Send your Holy Spirit upon us!
    Enable us to tell of your awesome power!

Opening Prayer

With your whole creation, O Lord our God, we long for redemption, we yearn for adoption, we hope in Christ for our salvation! Help us in our weakness by the power of your Spirit, for we do not know how to pray as we ought, and we need you to intercede for us according to your holy will!

Call to Confession

God alone has the power to breathe life into the dead, to redeem for vital service those who are otherwise lifeless due to the weighty burden of guilt and sin. This God who turns slaves into prophets, the young into visionaries, and the old into dreamers of the future glory, can be trusted with the truth about our sin.

Prayer of Confession

Spirit of the Living God, we confess that change fills our hearts with sorrow, loss stirs up doubt and fear, and our memories of past unfaithfulness often make life unbearable. Yet you are more than faithful in providing for us and for all creatures under heaven. You are good to renew all things with your Holy Spirit and to give countless blessings with your open and generous hand. Forgive us, O God, for our shortsightedness, our lack of faith, our timidity. Empower us with your Holy Spirit to proclaim your good works and to do your will in all things, for the sake of your Son Jesus Christ.

Declaration of Forgiveness

Surely all who call upon the name of the Lord will be saved! The God, who takes care to proclaim the gospel to all peoples in their mother tongue, has made provision for forgiveness for every believer under heaven and redemption for the whole of creation under the governance of Jesus Christ. Receive the good news, even as you receive anew the promised Holy Spirit, for in Jesus Christ we are forgiven!

Presentation of Tithes and Offerings

Make your best offerings to the Lord your God, the self-giving One! For in Christ, we see God's love poured out for us, and with the Holy Spirit, we have God's faithful and powerful presence living with us, watching over

us, working through us, and providing for us in wonderful abundance!
Bless the LORD with all your hearts, even as you offer your gifts of thanks!

PRAYER OF DEDICATION

We bless you, O God, for the ultimate gift of yourself to us, the inspiring,
empowering Spirit of life and truth! Even as we ask that the fires of godly
passion be fanned to roaring flames in our hearts, so bless these gifts also,
as we seek to use them for the spreading of your kingdom like wildfire!

THE BLESSING

Go in the power of the Holy Spirit
to spread the good news of Jesus Christ the Lord.
Go with the passion of your Savior, Christ Jesus,
to set your heart aflame in obedience and love.
Go in the love of God your Father
to stir you to compassion and keep you in faith!

PART III

Ordinary Time (Propers 4–29)
Trinity—All Saints'—Christ the King

Trinity Sunday

Isaiah 6:1–8

Psalm 29

Romans 8:12–17

John 3:1–17

In Preparation for Worship

So that our knowing should not be so narrow,
you, O God, have made yourself known
in glory, in thunder, in wind, in spirit,
in light, in sound, in breath, in bone,
in water, in flesh, in blood, in marrow.
Thank you, O Father, Son, Spirit,
for the fullness of your holy Oneness,
for the Oneness of your manifold nature!

Call to Worship

All who are led by the Spirit of God
are children of God!
Praise be to you, O Holy One!
For you have given us a spirit of adoption!
When we cry, "Abba! Father!" it is that very Spirit testifying
that we are children of God.
Praise be to you, O Holy One!
For you have made us joints heirs with Christ!
All who suffer in solidarity with Christ Jesus
are glorified with him!
Praise be to you, O Holy One in Three!
We gather in your most blessed name!

135

Opening Prayer

We long to live eternally with you, O God! Send forth your Holy Spirit, that we may be born from above, healed in Christ, raised to new life in your loving presence, for you are one in mind, one in will, one in purpose, our triune God!

Call to Confession

How shall we ascribe glory to the LORD, if we fail to fear God's holiness? How shall we fear God's holiness, if we fail to acknowledge our sin? With fear and trembling, let us express to God our dismay at our own sin, and our dissatisfaction with ourselves as participants in the sins of the world.

Prayer of Confession

Holy God, we confess that we live unclean lives among unclean people. Unless you touch us we are lost, unless you save us we are condemned. Yet you have declared that your purpose in sending Christ Jesus is not for condemnation, but for our salvation, and this salvation is not only for us, but for the whole world! Free us, O God, from our countless fears. Forgive us, O LORD, for our tendency toward the flesh. Impart to us your Holy Spirit, that Christ might be formed in us for your glory and majesty and honor!

Declaration of Forgiveness

Whenever the power of sin threatens you, wherever the curse of sin touches you, God has raised up a divine healer to whom you can turn for salvation! The healer is Christ, who takes our deeds of the flesh and deposits them in death on our behalf. Fear not! Be assured! Your healing is yours in the moment of your turning in faith to the Christ, who has been crucified for your salvation and raised up again, that you may receive the gift of eternal life!

Presentation of Tithes and Offerings

As joint heirs of God, joint heirs with Christ Jesus, we know that the resources of this world belong first, and last, and for all time, to the One who created them, our holy God! We also know that our use of God's resources is a sacred trust of familial responsibility and loving devotion.

Therefore, let us dedicate a portion of God's resources that have come into our care to the ministry of God's people, yielding them to the power of the Holy Spirit and in obedience to Christ.

PRAYER OF DEDICATION

Ever-faithful God, you are holy, righteous, and loving. We seek to live in a manner worthy of your name and of people whom you have called to be your children. Help us, our Father, as we devote these gifts to you, to administer them faithfully in your name, to be ever more conformed to the image of your Son and to your holy intentions for us! Help us, O Christ, to emulate your self-emptying generosity. Help us, O enlivening Spirit, to manifest in our surrender of these blessings, and to recognize in your righteous direction of their use, the sovereignty of our triune God!

THE BLESSING

May the blood of Jesus seal you,
the Holy Spirit fill you,
and the angel of the LORD encamp around you,
as you commit your life to our holy God!

Proper 4
Ordinary Time 9 / May 29–June 4 (*if after Trinity*)

1 Samuel 3:1–10 (11–20)

Psalm 139:1–6, 13–18

2 Corinthians 4:5–12

Mark 2:23—3:6

IN PREPARATION FOR WORSHIP

O Inescapable God,
your eyes see through me,
your mind understands me
better than I understand myself.
I cannot flee from you, therefore I will seek you,
for you are acquainted with all my ways.

CALL TO WORSHIP

Come, all who long to hear a word from the LORD!
Let none of God's words fall to the ground!
Speak to us, O God. For we, your servants, are listening.
Come, all who have heard God's call in the night!
Let none of God's words be forgotten!
Speak to us, O God. For we, your servants, are listening.
Come, all who would do the LORD's bidding! Attend to the Word of God!
Speak to us, O God. We seek the bread of your true presence.

Opening Prayer

Lord of the Sabbath, you have created us and gifted us with this day of rest to remind us that you are ever with us and we are ever in you. Feed us now with the bread of your word, anoint and fill us with your Holy Spirit, make your life visible in our mortal bodies, that you might be known among us and your glory might be renowned throughout the world!

Call to Confession

The laws of God are given as a grace, a gift that describes for us a blessed life and prescribes the behaviors which, when practiced, promote our health and that of our neighbor. Rather than allowing the law to do its work for us until we are mature and responsible enough to live in the spirit in which it was given, we rebel against the law, mistaking it for an enemy, not a friend to our freedom. We hold it out to show others their shortcomings, while we too have failed to measure up to its demand that we become our best. Let us confess our transgressions of God's laws, even as we appeal through Christ for forgiveness and reconciliation, and ask to be restored under the rule of grace.

Prayer of Confession

Holy God, in Jesus Christ your word has reached into this world that is so full of sin, depravity, and death. We confess that we have turned a deaf ear to you, tried to flee from your Spirit, and disobeyed your commandments of love. Restore and refresh us, God of mercy. Let your grace overtake us wherever we are. Shine your light into our hearts, that we might know your glory in Jesus Christ and proclaim him to the world as Lord of all.

Declaration of Forgiveness

Beloved in Christ, hear these words of hope! Though we be afflicted in every way, we are not crushed. Though we be perplexed, we are not driven to despair. Though we be persecuted and struck down, we are neither forsaken nor destroyed. Though we carry in our bodies the death of Jesus, nevertheless, the life of Jesus is made visible in our mortal flesh. Take heart! For the treasure we have in these clay jars is the extraordinary power of God! Let the light of God shine in your hearts, who has called you from darkness into the knowledge of the glory of Christ!

Presentation of Tithes and Offerings

What earthly blessings can compare with the rich treasure of knowing the God who is ever present with us, of knowing our Savior, Jesus Christ the Lord? Let us free ourselves for a deeper knowledge of God by giving as God gives!

Prayer of Dedication

In your awesome presence, O Holy One, we return these treasures to you. Receive our humble act of thanks and praise and our heartfelt plea that you would render us holy along with these gifts, that all might be used to honor your name!

The Blessing

Go with your Creator, who knew you before the beginning; follow the Christ, who anticipates your every move; remain in the Spirit, who will work wonders through you; and the triune God be with you to the end!

Proper 5
Ordinary Time 10 / June 5–11 (*if after Trinity*)

1 Samuel 8:4–11 (12–15) 16–20 (11:14–15)

Psalm 138

2 Corinthians 4:13—5:1

Mark 3:20–35

IN PREPARATION FOR WORSHIP

We bless your mighty name, O God,
for we have heard your gracious word!
We seek your presence, O Holy One,
for you raise us in Christ toward our heavenly home!
We long for your Spirit of renewal, O LORD,
in hopes of reaching our eternal reward!

CALL TO WORSHIP

Silence vain speech and wordy diffusion.
Join your voices in praise of God.
> **Give thanks to the LORD with a full heart.**
> **For great is the glory of the LORD our God!**
Arise from out of all strife and confusion.
Unite your hearts in the Spirit of God.
> **Bow before the LORD of heaven and earth.**
> **Sing of the wonderful ways of God!**
Put away your ambitions like so much illusion.
Adopt Christ's vision of the kingdom of God.
> **The rulers of the earth will bless the LORD.**
> **For Christ our LORD is ruler over all!**

Opening Prayer

We praise you and we bless you, O God our Creator, for you have regarded your lowly people. You have delivered us in times of trouble, and answered us when we have cried out to you. You are steadfast in your love and constant in your mercy. Fulfill your purpose for us, O God. Do not forsake the work of your hands!

Call to Confession

Though the visible record of our sins testifies against us, the invisible God preserves the humble and regards the lowly, while remaining distant from the haughty and the arrogant, those who think they have no sin to confess. Therefore, let us bow before and submit to the judgments of our God, as is seemly of humble people of faith.

Prayer of Confession

Holy One, you have called us to be united in doing your will, and in this way to be your family. Yet we create dissension and suffer division, we conform to comfortable, empty traditions, and we remain under the influence of the same unclean spirits from which you would set us free. Cleanse us, free us, forgive us, O Lord! Fill us with your Holy Spirit of renewal. Increase our strength of soul. Regard your lowly servants, and unite us in the sacred work of your eternal kingdom!

Declaration of Forgiveness

Let grace increase thanksgiving to the glory of God. The One who raised the Lord Jesus from the dead will raise us also with Jesus. The difficulties of the present are but a slight momentary affliction by which we are being prepared for an eternal weight of glory beyond all measure. Keep faith in the Lord who is gracious and good, for God's steadfast love endures forever.

Presentation of Tithes and Offerings

Everything has been done for the sake of your salvation. In Christ we have our building from God, an eternal, heavenly dwelling place. Therefore, give thanks to God with your whole heart. Do the will of God with a grateful attitude, that the glory of God might be evident in your joy and your generosity!

PRAYER OF DEDICATION

Sovereign God, we believe that you have a holy purpose for us, a redeeming work that we would ask you to fulfill through us, even as you bring us to maturity. Consecrate these goods with your sabbatical spirit that we and they may play our respective roles in your holy order and show forth the glory of your new creation.

THE BLESSING

You are the children of the Most High God.
You are the family of Jesus Christ, the Ruler of all creation.
You are sacred vessels of the Holy Spirit.
So take up your noble calling:
Be a blessing to the LORD and to your neighbors;
do God's will in everything, and live in peace.

Proper 6
Ordinary Time 11 / June 12–18 (*if after Trinity*)

1 Samuel 15:34—16:13

Psalm 20

2 Corinthians 5:6–10 (11–13) 14–17

Mark 4:26–34

In Preparation for Worship

Though we live in the body, O great God of heaven,
we would rather be at home with you!
Though we cannot see you,
we approach in faith to worship you!
Preserve us, O Spirit; renew and re-create us,
that we might live eternally with you!

Call to Worship

Come to the Lord and offer up your praises.
Take pride in the name of the Lord alone.
   We have every confidence in you, O God.
   For you enable us to walk by faith.
Set up your banners in the name of the Lord.
Shout for joy over your victory in God!
   Christ has died for all; therefore, all have died.
   Let us live no longer for ourselves, but for Christ.
Rise and stand upright, all you who bear the name of Christ.
For the Lord will help and vindicate the anointed.
   Answer us when we call, O God.
   Answer us from your holy heaven!

Opening Prayer

Spirit of the Living God, you give growth and life and energy to your kingdom in ways that we do not fully comprehend. Therefore, we gladly trust in you for your vital provisions. Grant, O Lord, our heart's desire, as we seek to fulfill your plans for us. Hear and answer our petitions, O Christ, for without you we can do nothing!

Call to Confession

How very well known we are to God, who sees and hears and observes us at every stage of our growth and life. All of us must appear before the judgment seat of Christ, so that each may receive compensation for what has been done in the body, whether good or evil. Knowing, then, that we must answer to Christ, from whom we can hide nothing, let us not commend ourselves for anything, but let us confess all that would otherwise testify against us, that we might surrender the former ways, unburden our hearts, and cleanse our consciences before the Lord.

Prayer of Confession

God of Grace and Truth, we admit that we do not see as you see. We judge people by surface appearances and vague impressions, when we really have no business judging at all. In doing so, we reveal to you, our true judge of the heart, our need to be cleansed from sinful ways and created anew in Christ. Set us free, O Loving God! Help us, O God, to let our old nature die, to regard others from your point of view, to make it our true aim in all things to please you!

Declaration of Forgiveness

Beloved, take courage in this: Christ has died for all; therefore, all have died. Let us no longer live for ourselves, but let us live for the One who died and was raised for us! If you are in Christ, you are a new creation: everything old has passed away! See, everything has become new! Therefore, let the love of Christ renew you, re-create you, and urge you on, as you serve the Savior with your new being!

Presentation of Tithes and Offerings

The kingdom of God is such that our God grows the seeds we sow, God blesses the work we do, and God broadens the sphere of our outreach, even after we have completed our share in the work and gone on to other things. But, as participants with God in the process of kingdom building, we must do our part by planting seeds and placing our gifts in the hands of God.

Prayer of Dedication

With the offering of these gifts to you, O Lord of Life, let new seeds be sown for the growth of your kingdom, the spreading of your word, the glory of your Anointed One, Jesus Christ, in whose name we give you thanks and praise.

The Blessing

Go with faith in God to guide you, and Christ to give you new life in the Spirit!

Proper 7
Ordinary Time 12 / June 19–25 (*if after Trinity*)

1 Samuel 17:(1a, 4–11, 19–23) 32–49 OR 1 Samuel 17:57—18:5, 10–16
Psalm 9:9–20 OR Psalm 133
2 Corinthians 6:1–13
Mark 4:35–41

IN PREPARATION FOR WORSHIP

Lord of the elements,
as you calmed the wind and sea,
still us with your Holy Spirit,
bear us through your baptismal waters,
and set us safely ashore on a sure and certain faith.

CALL TO WORSHIP

Those who seek the LORD will not be forsaken.
The cry of the afflicted will not go unheard.
Those who forget God are caught in their own nets.
The nations sink in the pits they dig for others.
Those in need will not be forgotten.
The LORD will be our stronghold and stay.
Lift up your people in their time of need, O God!
Then we shall rejoice and sing your praise!

OPENING PRAYER

O God our Deliverer, who answers the taunts of the arrogant, you brought
down the giant by the hand of your humble servant David. Surely there is

no enemy too great for you. Therefore, we laud your deeds of power and praise your holy name, O God our Deliverer.

Call to Confession

Let not one of us accept the grace of God in vain. God's grace in Jesus Christ is costly grace, not cheap. Therefore, open wide your hearts for the Lord to examine. Share your struggles, frustrations, and imperfections with God, and know the healing power of Christ's costly gift for your growth and forgiveness.

Prayer of Confession

Creator God, we confess we are often anxious, for we experience the destructive forces of sin. Through pride we cause innocents to suffer, through fear we perpetuate untold pain. Speak your word once again to the troubled winds and waters. Calm our stormy lives with your peaceful presence. Make peace to reign where we have earned your reproach, so that we might live again under your rule of grace and gratitude, in Jesus' name.

Declaration of Forgiveness

Now is the day of salvation! Now is the acceptable time! Christ is sovereign over all creation. Even the wind and sea obey him! Therefore, set your minds at rest. God has chosen you to experience his grace and freedom in the Holy Spirit. Therefore, harbor no more fear, but make room for faith, felicity, and peace, in Jesus' name.

Presentation of Tithes and Offerings

Even when we have nothing, as servants of God, we possess everything! What more can we want than to know and be known by Christ? Though we be poor, we make many rich by sharing in the love, the grace, and the fellowship of God. Let us share boldly, generously, joyfully, in gratitude for our salvation.

Prayer of Dedication

We offer you these gifts, O God, with open hands and open hearts. May no restrictions in our affections limit your power to impart the grace of giving, the life of loving, or the benefits your Spirit brings.

The Blessing

Do not fear the storms of life, for Christ himself is in your boat.
Do not fail to trust in God to see you through the trials of living.
Do not face the world without the Spirit to guide you in the ways of peace.

Proper 8
Ordinary Time 13 / June 26–July 2

2 Samuel 1:1, 17–27

Psalm 130

2 Corinthians 8:7–15

Mark 5:21–43

IN PREPARATION FOR WORSHIP

Holy Lord,
you touch the unclean and make them clean;
you make the dead to rise.
Come again among your unworthy people,
and redeem us for your glory.

CALL TO WORSHIP

Out of the depths I cry to you, O LORD!
> **LORD, hear our voice!**
If you, O LORD, should mark iniquities—
> **LORD, who could stand?**
The LORD's anointed has died upon the hillside.
> **The throne of David is established in power!**
Wait for the LORD, and hope in God's word!
> **With the LORD there is steadfast love, and great power to redeem.**

OPENING PRAYER

Savior of the World, you surrendered your human life and your divine wealth, becoming humble and poor, that we might be enlivened and enriched. Therefore, we praise you, eager to emulate your grace, earnestly wanting to share your love with all the world. Come to us, we pray, as we come to you, for the time for worship is now, and you are our glorious God!

Call to Confession

No one can stand in the presence of a holy God, unless God desires and permits it. If God's purpose was to punish every sin, we would never have survived the sins of our youth. But God's love for us is greater than all the sin we carry in us, mightier than all the sins we will ever conceive. In confession, give all your sin to God—sins of the past, present, and future—for God knows exactly what to do with sin.

Prayer of Confession

Healing God, you do not demand our perfection before you find us acceptable, but you come to us in our darkness and isolation, you meet us even in our sin. We admit our need for you to banish our demons and our diseases, to restore us with your gentle touch, to give us a new lease on life. Pardon us for the wrongs we have done, and increase our faith in our resurrected Lord, that we might participate in the resurrection life.

Declaration of Forgiveness

God alone sets the people free from all their sin. God alone can take the unholy and make it holy, infiltrating sin with hope and love. This is precisely how God saves human beings through Jesus Christ. In Christ God became human, getting under the weight of human sin with us, transforming fallen creatures into spirit-filled disciples, preparing a fallen creation for the coming reign of heaven. Therefore, the LORD is to be revered! Receive the grace and the hope of God!

Presentation of Tithes and Offerings

If we are eager to give, then our gifts, no matter how rich or poor we are, are acceptable to God. Jesus is our great example. He was not materially wealthy, but as the Son of God, he was exceedingly rich. He chose to become poor, so that those who trust in him might share in his eternal riches. Let us eagerly make our gifts acceptable to God, the great Giver!

Prayer of Dedication

You could claim all that we have, anytime you chose, O God. Yet you graciously wait for us to offer, and then you give to us in return. We thank you, Lord, for your unending cycle of giving, as we remember our part in that cycle. We offer these treasures, come from you, now returned to you, that you might bless them, and your people in their use.

The Blessing

Go in peace, freed by Christ from the power of death.
Go in grace, free to obey the leading of the Spirit.
Go in love, free to love your Creator with all your heart.

Proper 9
Ordinary Time 14 / July 3–9

2 Samuel 5:1–5, 9–10

Psalm 48

2 Corinthians 12:2–10

Mark 6:1–13

IN PREPARATION FOR WORSHIP

In your heavenly courts we are humbled.
In your holy presence we are weak.
In weakness and humility,
we draw near to you
to draw upon your strength.

CALL TO WORSHIP

The LORD is great and greatly to be praised!
> **We will meditate on the steadfast love
> and mercy of the LORD.**
God's holy mountain is the joy of all the earth!
> **We will praise God's holy name
> in the midst of his temple.**
Consider the strength and beauty of Zion!
> **God will be our guide forever and ever.**

OPENING PRAYER

O God, you are our guide and provider. You lead us to those who accept
and welcome us in the name of Christ. By your grace we have each other;

by your giving we have plenty to share. As we gather to devote our hearts, our minds, our hands, and our lives to you, so use us that the world might come to know you through the service we render, in Jesus' name.

CALL TO CONFESSION

The Lord Jesus Christ has promised that his grace is sufficient for the weak. We have no hope but in God's grace, yet what more hope do we need? The same Jesus who experienced rejection by his own people, will not reject those who approach him with remorse for sin and trust in his goodness. Bring your sins to the God who governs by grace, and surrender them at the altar of peace.

PRAYER OF CONFESSION

Almighty and Merciful God, we have many thorns in our flesh, countless vulnerabilities and vices. We operate according to mixed motives, rationalizing our many faults and making scapegoats of others when we feel threatened or exposed by them. Forgive us, O God, by your abundant grace, and permit us to draw ever nearer to you in holiness and truth, in Jesus' name.

DECLARATION OF FORGIVENESS

God is your protector, a sure defense against all who would accuse or condemn you. Christ is your strength, sharing with you the longings and struggles of all humanity, yet offering you the very power of the Holy Spirit and the compassion of the heavenly Father to see you through your trials, your failures, your new beginnings. Receive the grace and strength of Christ to supplant your guilt and weakness, for in Christ we are empowered and forgiven.

PRESENTATION OF TITHES AND OFFERINGS

Jesus told his disciples to take nothing with them but a walking staff: no bread, no bag, no money in their belts. The success of their mission depended on their trust in God to provide for their needs, and on the generosity and hospitality of those who would receive their gospel message and welcome them in the name of the Lord. Let us trust in God, as did those first evangelists, and respond to the gospel with hospitable hearts and open hands, as did their receptive hosts!

PRAYER OF DEDICATION

What we do with our wealth is a measure of our trust in you, O God. Receive this measure, this expression of faith and devotion. Bless, consecrate, and multiply it, for we would proclaim your reign by our speech, our prayers, our thoughts, and our actions, in Jesus' name.

THE BLESSING

May God your Provider meet all your needs.
May God your Redeemer remit all your debts.
May God your Inspirer fill you with the Spirit of love and truth,
grace and peace, in the name of Jesus Christ.

Proper 10
Ordinary Time 15 / July 10–16

2 Samuel 6:1–5, 12b–19

Psalm 24

Ephesians 1:3–14

Mark 6:14–29

IN PREPARATION FOR WORSHIP

Blessed God,
you have chosen us in Christ
to stand before you in love.
Beloved Christ, in you we are adopted.
Holy Spirit, you are the pledge of our inheritance.
We live for the praise of your glory!

CALL TO WORSHIP

Lift up your hearts,
for the ark of the LORD's might is revealed among his chosen people!
Praise the LORD, for our joy is restored!
Lift up your heads,
for your saving God comes to meet you!
Praise the LORD, for his glory is among us!
Raise your spirits,
for the redeeming God calls you to inherit salvation!
Let us worship God, for our lives are made new in Christ!

OPENING PRAYER

Almighty God, who blessed Israel with the ark of the covenant and returned it to them when it was captured, you have won the mighty victory for your people! With shouts of joy and songs of glad adoration, we thank you for your faithfulness in setting your throne in the midst of your people, whom you have called to be holy, priestly, and blameless before you. Help us, we pray, to always give honor to your Son, Jesus Christ, whom you have seated at your right hand! In his name we pray.

CALL TO CONFESSION

Who may approach the holy mountain of the LORD? Those who have clean hands and a pure heart, who set their hearts on truth. They shall receive a blessing from the LORD. Let us ask God to cleanse us from our sins, to wash our hands and purify our hearts. We do so by truthfully admitting our need for forgiveness and renewal to the One who readily gives these great gifts.

PRAYER OF CONFESSION

Loving God, you have created us to live for your praise and glory. Yet we, your Church, confess that we often trip one another up with harsh judgments, unfair criticism, unreasonable expectations, and all manner of abuse. We do not honor one another as we should, and when we fail to do so, we dishonor you. Forgive us for our sins of omission and commission, that we might be made holy and blameless in your sight, and once again praise your glory.

DECLARATION OF FORGIVENESS

Scripture assures us that God's grace is lavished on us. Through grace, we are forgiven, redeemed, and enriched. So take your freedom in Christ, gather up your spiritual riches, live in joy, grow in grace, abound with thanksgiving, for your past memories, your present salvation, and your future inheritance are all in the hands of our blessed and loving Lord!

PRESENTATION OF TITHES AND OFFERINGS

The world belongs to the One who created it, the LORD's creatures to the One who gave them birth. All the treasures of this earth, yes, every thing belongs to the LORD, and all is ours to share with the whole of creation. Let us share with God what he has so openly shared with us.

PRAYER OF DEDICATION

Almighty God, no enemy can take away your glory, no violence can extort the integrity of your faithful servants. May we use these treasures to serve you with integrity, to the increase of your glory, even in the face of the enemies of sharing.

THE BLESSING

May you who believe the word of truth
be ever marked with the seal of the Holy Spirit.
May all things in heaven and earth
be gathered up in Jesus Christ.
May you who are called to glorify God
be enriched with every spiritual blessing!

Proper 11
Ordinary Time 16 / July 17–23

2 Samuel 7:1–14a

Psalm 89:20–37

Ephesians 2:11–22

Mark 6:30–34, 53–56

In Preparation for Worship

O God, who created the world for peace;
O Christ, whose throne endures like the sun;
O Spirit, who reconciles every nation and race:
may our heartfelt worship of you begin.

Call to Worship

Come away to a desert place,
> **for God is not contained in houses of cedar!**
Come away to a desert place,
> **for God is the rock of our salvation!**
Christ is our peace!
> **Through Jesus Christ, we have access to God in the Holy Spirit.**
> **Therefore, as Christ's body, let us unite to worship God!**

Opening Prayer

God of the covenant, in Jesus Christ you have broken down the walls of
hostility that have kept us apart from your chosen people. By your grace,

we are no longer alienated from you. Now build us together in your own Holy Spirit, that we might be your dwelling place.

CALL TO CONFESSION

We remember that, at one time, we were without Christ, unknown to God's promises to Israel. But it is by Christ's blood that we are brought near, and it is in the cross that Jews and Gentiles are made one, divisions are healed, and peace is proclaimed. Let us confess our sin and our need of this reconciliation.

PRAYER OF CONFESSION

God of Peace, we regret that we have not been peacemakers. We have trusted in our differences to define and delimit us, and we have misused our gifts to build ourselves up and to tear each other down. Grant us your pardon and give us your peace, that we might know the joy of reuniting with all the saints and the members of your holy household.

DECLARATION OF FORGIVENESS

Wherever Jesus went, those who simply reached out to him were healed. As you have reached out to Christ in confession, may you also know renewal, refreshment, and forgiveness from our compassionate Savior, our healing Lord. Take this good news into every hurting place: In Jesus Christ, we are forgiven!

PRESENTATION OF TITHES AND OFFERINGS

As members of one household share the burdens and the property of the entire house, so it is with the members of the household of God. We share and bear with one another in the Spirit of Christ. So offer your gifts to the LORD, for the joy of God's family in heaven, and for the well-being of God's family on earth.

PRAYER OF DEDICATION

Self-giving God, when Jesus and the disciples needed to rest, still they made provision for those in need. May we learn to do likewise. Where we have been quick to list our own needs, convict us. Where we have been slow to respond to the needs of others, convert us. May this offering be a testimony to our new and ever deeper trust in you, that your name might be glorified by the generosity and caring of your people.

THE BLESSING

You have reached out to God.
Now remain in touch with your Creator.
You have touched the garment of Christ.
Now carry his healing Spirit into the world with you.
You have the Holy Spirit alive in you.
Now live every moment in love with God.

Proper 12
Ordinary Time 17 / July 24–30

2 Samuel 11:1–15

Psalm 14

Ephesians 3:14–21

John 6:1–21

IN PREPARATION FOR WORSHIP

Glorious God,
fill us with your fullness,
strengthen us in our inner being,
give us the power to comprehend, with all the saints,
what is the breadth and length, the height and depth
of the love of Christ, surpassing all knowledge.

CALL TO WORSHIP

Christ feeds us, even in the wilderness!
Let us be filled with the fullness of God!
Christ changes us, from a grasping to a sharing people.
We will be satisfied with the bread of heaven!
Christ loves us, dwelling in our hearts through faith.
Let us be rooted and grounded in love!
Let us worship God!
Alleluia! Amen!

Opening Prayer

God of power and glory, you are able to accomplish within us far more than we can ask or imagine. You have the power to multiply a few modest loaves and fishes into a feast for five thousand. Work your miracles within our hearts this day, that your glory may be seen and known in the Church, for the sake of Christ Jesus our Lord.

Call to Confession

All we like sheep have gone astray. There is not one among us who is good, in and of ourselves. As God looks down from heaven, what does the Lord see? Fools who say there is no God! How shall we answer God for all our sins? Not by hiding them, but by seeking after God, despite our sinfulness—by owning up to the evil inside us, and trusting in our loving Lord to remove all sin from our penitent hearts.

Prayer of Confession

Merciful God, we have violated your trust. We have clung to the provisions you have entrusted to us, envied our neighbors, and sought satisfaction at their expense. Reconcile us with one another, with you, and with all your creation, that our instinct might be to care for one another in your Spirit of love and to share your abundant blessings with those who are lost, searching, and needing an encounter with your grace.

Declaration of Forgiveness

The Lord is our refuge! God is present in the company of the righteous! By his grace we are made righteous in the act of confession. Therefore, have faith! Trust in the gospel of forgiveness, for the Lord is able and willing to do infinitely more than we can ask or imagine. Know that, in Christ, you are not only forgiven, you are abundantly blessed!

Presentation of Tithes and Offerings

As our Lord gave thanks to God, in the presence of five thousand, for the few provisions they had to share, so let us offer to God our gifts in thanksgiving. Be they few or be they many, they are ours from God, given to us that we might share.

PRAYER OF DEDICATION

God of miracles, regardless of our apprehension or appreciation, your blessings are ever before us. You give to us out of your deep storehouse of love and joy and peace. Receive this small fraction of all that we have from you, as we devote it, and our hearts, to your work in the world. Increase our awareness of all that we have to enjoy, to share, and to use, so that our life in you and with you might reflect the favor of your presence at work among your people.

THE BLESSING

God is a God of plenty and joy!
So see with new eyes your Creator's many blessings.
Christ is a God of trust and vulnerability!
So feel with a new heart Christ's openness and love.
The Holy Spirit is a God of wisdom and power!
So receive with a new spirit God's guidance and strength.
Share all these things with those whom you meet.

Proper 13
Ordinary Time 18 / July 31–August 6

2 Samuel 11:26—12:13a

Psalm 51:1–12

Ephesians 4:1–16

John 6:24–35

In Preparation for Worship

Bread of Heaven, come down!
Give life to the world!
Bread of Life, come down,
that we might feed each other
and be filled!

Call to Worship

We see ourselves in the mirror of stories.
> **Now let us reflect upon the stories of God.**

We see our sin in the window of the Word.
> **Now let us be open to the prophecies of God.**

We see the way of salvation in Christ.
> **Come, Spirit of Christ, and open our eyes, change our minds,**
> **and warm our hearts as we gather to worship you**
> **and our Heavenly Father, in spirit and in truth.**

OPENING PRAYER

Living God of Justice and Truth, you have anointed us royally with your Spirit in the one baptism that unites us with Christ. You are quick to feed us richly with the bread of your Word. Therefore, make of us honest, humble, and gentle servants, united in love for the honor of your holy name.

CALL TO CONFESSION

God is just and blameless in passing judgment on human sin, for our sin haunts us from the day we are born. But God, who is merciful, can blot out our sin and create within each of us a clean heart, a right and a willing spirit. Do not wait to be found out, but lay your faults before God in confession, and let Christ reign over your conscience again.

PRAYER OF CONFESSION

Merciful God, you have favored us with many blessings, yet we confess that our eyes and our envy are often focused on what little our neighbors have. We admit our foolish discontent despite your goodness to us, our misuse of what power we have, and the destructive consequences of our sin. Save us, O God, from sin and from ourselves, that we might be free again to live in the love of Christ.

DECLARATION OF FORGIVENESS

God's mercy is abundant and thorough, instructive and healing. Receive into your hearts the joy and the peace of God's salvation! Christ has made captivity itself a captive. Therefore, you are free to sin no more, free to explore the wide world of obedience to God, united with Christ in the Spirit of love. May each of you grow, and encourage one another to grow, into the full stature of Christ Jesus, our gracious Lord.

PRESENTATION OF TITHES AND OFFERINGS

God has not only given us all that we need to live, but also the Spirit of life itself! Christ Jesus is the true bread of heaven, who gives life to the world. Whoever comes to Christ will never be hungry, and whoever believes in Christ will never thirst. Since God in Christ supplies all our needs, offer up your life and your living in dedication to God, and gather up your gifts to present before the LORD.

PRAYER OF DEDICATION

Gracious God, you have given us many, many gifts, all for the work of ministry and for building up the body of Christ. We thank you, God, and as we lift up to you that which you have given us, raise us up into the full stature of Christ. Lead us in a life worthy of our calling, for we have each received grace according to the measure of what Christ has given us.

THE BLESSING

Your God is above all, and in all, and through all!
Therefore, love all, and be humble and gentle and patient toward all.
Your Christ is the head of the body of the Church and Lord of all creation!
Therefore, build up the members of Christ's body and care for God's creatures.
You are all part of the one body and the one Spirit!
Therefore, make every effort to maintain the unity of the Spirit
in the bond of peace.

Proper 14
Ordinary Time 19 / August 7–13

2 Samuel 18:5–9, 15, 31–33

Psalm 130

Ephesians 4:25—5:2

John 6:35, 41–51

IN PREPARATION FOR WORSHIP

O God, you have marked us with your Holy Spirit
for the day of our redemption;
you have offered up the Christ
as a sacrifice for us.
Help us to respond in truth,
that we may worship you with love
and be gathered to you in unity and peace.

CALL TO WORSHIP

We assemble in the presence of the Holy God.
With God there is forgiveness,
so that our God might be revered!
Be vigilant for the LORD and wait,
more than those who watch for the morning.
The LORD will hear our supplications!
O my people, hope in the LORD!
The LORD will grant our requests
according to God's will for us.

Opening Prayer

Bread of Heaven, we cannot come to you until you call us; we cannot pray unless you teach us. Come down and fill us, O Holy Manna. O Living Bread, feed us with your truth.

Call to Confession

Come to Christ, if you are hungry to be honest. Come to Christ, if you are thirsty for the truth. Christ, the living bread of life, turns away no one who truly seeks eternal life. Indeed, the One who came down from God was given up in the flesh, so that those who trust in this living bread may have life forevermore.

Prayer of Confession

God of Mercy, we have not practiced peace as you yourself are peace; we have not forgiven others as you have forgiven us. Forgive us, and help us to surrender all bitterness, anger, slander, and falsehood. Help us to be imitators of your goodness, made known to us in Christ. Help us to abide in Christ and live in love as your beloved children.

Declaration of Forgiveness

All who hear God's call and allow themselves to be taught by God's word shall come to Christ. And none who come will be turned away. God does not keep track of our sins. Rather, in Christ's self-offering to God on our behalf, our sins are erased, for there is forgiveness with God, so that we might stand in God's presence and offer to our Creator our reverent worship and praise.

Presentation of Tithes and Offerings

Our God provides! From God we have not only the bread we eat in this life, but also the living bread, Jesus Christ, who makes our eternal life with God both a future possibility and a present reality. Shall we not trust such a God with all that we have? Indeed, let us share with God our treasures and provisions, and in so doing, manifest the reality of God's kingdom here on earth.

PRAYER OF DEDICATION

O God, who supplies all that we truly need for life and for eternal life, you are the source of our very being, the giver of all that we possess. As you have poured out your blessings upon us, we pour out our hearts to you in praise, offering these gifts in the spirit of love, so that others might be built up, and your name might be made known to this generation and to those that are to come.

THE BLESSING

Trust God to satisfy all your hungers.
Trust the Christ who turns no one away.
Trust the Spirit who has marked you for the day of your redemption,
and be imitators of God in all that you do.

Proper 15
Ordinary Time 20 / August 14–20

1 Kings 2:10–12; 3:3–14

Psalm 111

Ephesians 5:15–20

John 6:51–58

IN PREPARATION FOR WORSHIP

God of wisdom,
you see all that we do not see,
you know all that we do not know.
Give us understanding and wisdom to discern
good from evil, courage from fear,
your righteous will from every temptation,
that we may praise you
by being more like you.

CALL TO WORSHIP

Praise the LORD!
Give thanks to God with all your heart.
> **In the company of the righteous,**
> **we praise the LORD!**
God has redeemed his people.
Holy and awesome is your name, O LORD!
> **In the company of the righteous,**
> **we praise God's holy name!**

God is full of grace and mercy!
All are fed who fear the LORD!
> **In the company of the righteous,**
> **we shall praise God forevermore!**

OPENING PRAYER

God of Majesty, we approach you in all your goodness, for your deeds are mighty and faithful and just, and you are exceedingly good to us. Fill us with your Holy Spirit, that we may sing psalms and hymns to you, making melody with heart and voice to our Lord Jesus Christ.

CALL TO CONFESSION

We live in times when evil is all around us, and compared to God, the wisest and best of us are but little children. We cannot expect to live perfectly or to be perfected unless we ask the Almighty to put aside our mistakes and to teach, discipline, correct, and guide us on our way. Let us seek God's help in confession.

PRAYER OF CONFESSION

Righteous God, we admit that we have neither behaved wisely nor sought your will before our own. We confess to avoiding you rather than holding you in awe and reverence as we should. Forgive us, O God, and rectify us in your sight, as we, by your guiding wisdom, align our living to conform with your decrees for life the way it is meant to be lived in your holy kingdom.

DECLARATION OF FORGIVENESS

We have asked to be forgiven. Now let us live as forgiven people. We have asked for God's wisdom. Now let us live as those who are wise, making the most of the time. The will of God is that we should live in peace, and to give us this peace, God has arranged for our liberty by means of a new covenant sealed in the blood of Christ and in the Holy Spirit: Those who humble themselves and eat the living bread of Christ shall live forever. Know that you are forgiven and live at peace.

PRESENTATION OF TITHES AND OFFERINGS

Christ has offered to us, and to the Father on our behalf, his very flesh and blood. Such a liberal gift for our liberation demands we conserve unaltered the truth about it, and announce it to the world with utmost generosity! May the offerings we make this day help set us and others free! Let us dedicate ourselves anew to God—and, along with ourselves, all the life and health and wealth we have to give.

PRAYER OF DEDICATION

God of wisdom, we magnify you for who you are and praise your holy name! Yours is the wise counsel we seek and the example we desire to follow. In your Spirit of self-giving, we uplift heart and soul, mind and body, our flesh and blood, as did Jesus Christ. We thank you for the life and the liberty we have through him, trusting that these gifts will be used to draw others to him; in your holy name we pray.

THE BLESSING

Learn to adore God in the wisdom of simplicity.
Search for Christ in the fabric of creation.
Listen for the Spirit in the music of your heart,
and the peace of heaven will be yours to share!

Proper 16
Ordinary Time 21 / August 21–27

1 Kings 8: (1, 6, 10–11) 22–30, 41–43

Psalm 84

Ephesians 6:10–20

John 6:56–69

In Preparation for Worship

Eternal Spirit,
I clothe myself in you,
taking faith and righteousness,
peace and salvation as my whole armor,
and your word as my holy sword,
that I may stand against the powers of evil
and boldly proclaim the mystery of your message.

Call to Worship

Happy is everyone who trusts in the Lord!
Let us sing for joy to the living God!
O how I long for the presence of God!
**One day in your house is better than
a thousand elsewhere, O Lord!**
I would rather be a doorkeeper in the house of my God
than live in the tents of wickedness.
**How lovely is your dwelling place,
O Lord God of hosts!**

Happy are those who live in your house!
We shall sing your praise forever!

OPENING PRAYER

Holy LORD, you are truly amazing! There is no god like you in heaven or on the earth! You are the keeper of covenants, the savior of peoples known to us and of strangers near and far. Now, as we enter your holy dwelling place, knowing that no palace can contain you, no temple can domesticate the power of your holy name, receive our prayers and praises, O God, and look with favor upon all who worship you. Let the glory of your face shine upon us, in Jesus' name.

CALL TO CONFESSION

Only God can bridge the distance that separates us from his holiness. We rely upon him wholly and on the provision he has made for us in Christ Jesus for restoring us to a state of grace and godliness. Let us reach out to God.

PRAYER OF CONFESSION

Holy God, hear the plea of your people as we pray within this holy place. Hear us and forgive! For we have failed to keep your covenant, and we have broken your commandments. Yet even when we have tried to obey, we have easily been distracted, forgetful, and enticed by temptations to sin. Give us leave to live again, fully immersed in your faithful presence with us and in your living word, Jesus Christ, whom we know is on our side, ever leading us in the way of truth and love.

DECLARATION OF FORGIVENESS

When the disciples were discouraged, unable to understand Jesus' teachings, many turned away from him, and many others considered it. But when Jesus asked if they too would abandon him, Peter replied, "Lord, to whom shall we go? You have the words to eternal life." Indeed, there is no one else who is able to free us for eternal life, and though we do not always understand, yet we have learned to trust first, and then to seek greater understanding. Trust this message, and then seek to understand: In Jesus Christ, we are forgiven and we have eternal life.

PRESENTATION OF TITHES AND OFFERINGS

Even sparrows and swallows find a home at the altar of God, and those who find their strength in God go from strength to strength. Let us be as those who always trust in God for shelter and strength, presenting our desires and our needs, our lives and our bodies, our weakness as well as our strengths, all for God's use and redeeming. Let us entrust everything to God, our glorious provider!

PRAYER OF DEDICATION

As Solomon dedicated the great temple to you, so we dedicate these temples in which you dwell. We offer you the use and obedience of our bodies and minds, our gifts and energies, that you would renew and enrich them for lives of prayer and praise and perseverance in the faith. May all our many blessings be used to bless your holy name.

THE BLESSING

Surround and clothe yourselves with the whole armor of God!
Arm yourselves with the gospel word.
Transform your thinking with the sure promise of salvation in Christ.
And may the Spirit guide and shelter you, keeping you from all evil
and inspiring your souls to constant prayer and praise.

Proper 17
Ordinary Time 22 / August 28–September 3

Song of Solomon 2:8–13

Psalm 45:1–2, 6–9

James 1:17–27

Mark 7:1–8, 14–15, 21–23

In Preparation for Worship

Grant unto me your Spirit, O Lord.
Implant in me your holy Word.
Guard my heart from all sordidness; purge me of all wickedness.
Plant deep within me your seed of goodness,
that the life that grows within me might be your own.

Call to Worship

People of God, the Spirit has anointed you!
With the oil of gladness, God has blessed you!
Your throne, O God, endures forever!
People of God, the Christ has clothed you!
With royal robes, the Lord surrounds you!
You rule, O God, with equity and justice!
People of God, your God has given you song!
With joyful music, the Word pours himself into your hearts!
You are welcome, O Christ, to enter our hearts!
May your words of grace be forever on our lips!

Opening Prayer

We gather, O God, to praise your goodness, to engage in honest reflection, to lay our sins at the foot of the cross, to receive with delight all the good and perfect gifts that come from above, and to listen for your Spirit to guide us in works of love and mercy and caring. You have given us birth by your word of truth, so help us to fulfill your purpose.

Call to Confession

We have been stained by the world. Too often we simply agree with the teachings of God, but fall short of actually living them. When we fail to follow through our beliefs with faithful action, our religion is shown to be worthless and our hearts false. But if we sincerely ask God to reform our hearts with truth and integrity, how can the Spirit of Truth refuse us? Who better to rehabilitate sinners to the ways of truth than Jesus, who is Truth itself? Let us confess our sins together, asking for the gifts we know God is eager to give.

Prayer of Confession

Righteous God, we confess that we have paid lip service to you while our hearts have been far away; we have trusted more in human teaching than in your divine wisdom. Forgive us, O God. Remove all the evil that hides or resides in our hearts, so that your ways and your words of grace and truth may be firmly rooted in our lives.

Declaration of Forgiveness

Every generous act of giving, including forgiving itself, is from above. Every perfect gift comes from God, who forgives perfectly. In humility and meekness, welcome this word of God's saving grace and plant it firmly in your hearts. The same perfect law that condemns us in our disobedience, guides us into freedom when we obey. And the purpose of this law is perfected in the love of Christ. Jesus Christ gave his life not because the law demanded it, but because his love for you did. Receive his love, and enjoy your new freedom in Christ!

PRESENTATION OF TITHES AND OFFERINGS

If we give generously, it is because God is alive in us and moves us to give. God's will for us is not only that our gifts bear fruit for the kingdom, but that we ourselves become like Christ, counted among the first fruits of the harvest. Bring your offerings to God and offer them from your hearts, so that your hearts might be full of goodness and, by your living, you might be a blessing to the world.

PRAYER OF DEDICATION

These gifts, O God, we offer from the inside, hoping and praying that, as we offer them for your holy works, you might find our hearts are also pure. Where our motives are false, forgive us and refine our gifts. Where they are true, give light to your world by the glory of Christ, in whose name we dedicate our lives to you.

THE BLESSING

Be quick to listen for the Holy Spirit!
Be reverent in your choice of words!
Be compassionate toward the lonely and the suffering,
and may Christ be ever in your hearts.

Proper 18
Ordinary Time 23 / September 4–10

Proverbs 22:1–2, 8–9, 22–23
Psalm 125
James 2:1–10 (11–13) 14–17
Mark 7:24–37

IN PREPARATION FOR WORSHIP

Holy Living Word,
open our ears so that we might hear you;
open our hearts so that we might love;
open our mouths so that we might praise you;
open heaven's doors and come down from above!

CALL TO WORSHIP

Those who trust in the LORD are like Holy Mount Zion:
They shall not be moved!
As the mountains protect Jerusalem,
God surrounds the faithful!
Those who trust in God will act on their trust.
They shall not turn aside from the needs of others.
As the righteous refuse to be governed by evil,
God will bless the upright in heart!
Those who are generous are blessed by God.
They will share their bread with the poor.
As goodness governs the hearts of the humble,
may peace be upon us as we worship our God!

Opening Prayer

God of Justice, you have chosen the people of Israel for your own, yet in Christ you have opened the doors to all. Satisfy us with the crumbs from your table, so that rich and poor, Jew and Gentile, might be reconciled to each other and to you.

Call to Confession

Faith without works is dead. Too often we say what we believe and stop short of real action, real change. How can our faith be a living faith if we do not trust it enough to act on it, if we do not believe enough to commit our time, our energy, our hope, our effort? Let us entrust the God of the resurrection with any deadness in our faith, by confessing our need to be made alive again.

Prayer of Confession

God of Grace and Mercy, we confess that we frequently judge other people, favoring the rich and beautiful, dishonoring the poor and heavily burdened. We ask you to forgive us and to awaken our senses to the good that we can do. Revive our living faith and stir us to righteous action, so that our trust in you might be evident to the world in the hospitality that we practice and the service we perform in Jesus' name.

Declaration of Forgiveness

If we are merciful, we shall be shown mercy. If we are forgiving, we shall be forgiven. Insofar as we are humble and honest, admitting our inability to save ourselves, God will save us with godly power. Friends, know that God's mercy triumphs over judgment. May your lives be changed by this news of God's grace: By grace through the faith of Christ you are saved and set free for works of love.

Presentation of Tithes and Offerings

A good name and a godly reputation cannot be bought. But we are blessed when we share our provisions with the poor. As we dedicate our gifts, let us devote our hearts to generous works of love in the name of Jesus Christ.

Prayer of Dedication

O Christ, you have done everything well. As we seek to live in you, to be a living part of you, and to do good works in your name, we ask that you would purify and increase these gifts with your holy grace, even as you fill our hearts with your Holy Spirit, so that their use would be a blessing to your kingdom and a winsome gift to those in need.

The Blessing

The blessings of God extend to you,
covering you with the covenant and offering you bread.
The faith of Christ is alive in you,
opening your ears to the needs of those around you.
The power of the Spirit is brimming inside you,
urging and encouraging you to share all that God has done for you!
Now go in peace to love and serve the Lord.

Proper 19
Ordinary Time 24 / September 11–17

Proverbs 1:20–33

Psalm 19

James 3:1–12

Mark 8:27–38

IN PREPARATION FOR WORSHIP

Creator God and Risen Christ,
Spirit of Truth and Inspiration,
your loving Word is the blessed message,
spoken for the saving of this dying world.
Equip us in this heavenly hour to become your blessed messengers.

CALL TO WORSHIP

The tongue is a flame: It can praise or it can destroy,
it can bless or it can curse.
> **Let us offer prayers in praise of God!**
> **Let us bless, and not curse, the children of God.**

The mind is a door. It can be open or it can be shut.
It can welcome or it can refuse.
> **Let us open our minds to the mind of Christ.**
> **Let us set our minds on the wisdom from above.**

May all our words and all our thoughts be acceptable to you,
O Lord, our rock and our redeemer!
> **Let us sing songs in praise of Jesus.**
> **Let us proclaim him Christ the Lord!**

OPENING PRAYER

Long-suffering God, as openly as the heavens tell of your glory, so you once openly foretold all that Christ would suffer for us. May we now also boldly declare, with our dying to self and our living for you, that our lives are in Christ Jesus, our crucified, risen, and sovereign Lord!

CALL TO CONFESSION

Who do you say that Jesus is? When we confess that Jesus is the Christ, God's own beloved and begotten Son, we also confess our need for this holy, godly one to save us. Christ has long been expected to save God's people. But it is only when we admit the depth of our sin that we also begin to appreciate how very much we are in need of a Savior. Let us admit our need and surrender to Christ.

PRAYER OF CONFESSION

Holy Word of God, you have made your will known, yet we often ignore your counsel. So much of our distress and despair is due to our having resisted you. Forgive us, O God, and form us anew. Create in us such a love for your Word that we might not be able to keep silent about your goodness, in Jesus' name.

DECLARATION OF FORGIVENESS

When we lay down our lives in confession, we pick them up again in forgiveness. But the life we take up again is a very different life from the one we lay down. For when we lay down the old life of sin, it dies! And we receive forgiveness, but with an entirely new purpose for living: to explore the vast reaches of God's kingdom. In Christ, the opportunity is yours again to choose and know the joys of holy living. You are forgiven. Be at peace.

PRESENTATION OF TITHES AND OFFERINGS

What can we give in return for our lives? Nothing! But do not let that stop you from giving out of gratefulness for the sake of the gospel! Each act of giving is a laying down of our lives for the sake of Christ's life within us. Each act of sharing is a proclamation that Jesus is Lord! Therefore, let us give, and let our giving be our proclamation.

PRAYER OF DEDICATION

Receive our wordless praise in the gesture of surrendering these portions to you. Declare your living Word in the joy we harbor within our hearts. Inspire this people to tell of your glory through the sharing we do this day. We ask this in Jesus' name.

THE BLESSING

The heavens are telling of the glory of God.
Add your voice to the voice of the heavens!
The Church proclaims that Jesus is the Christ.
Add your voice to the voice of the Church!
The inspired tongue speaks only truth and blessing.
Add your voice to the tongues of the Spirit!
And may you never be ashamed of the gospel.

Proper 20
Ordinary Time 25 / September 18–24

Proverbs 31:10–31

Psalm 1

James 3:13–4:3, 7–8a

Mark 9:30–37

In Preparation for Worship

O God, who watches over the way of the righteous,
we come as sinners to be made clean.
O Christ, who cleanses the repentant sinner,
we come to drink of your living streams.
O Spirit, who satisfies the thirst of God's children,
fill us with your righteous peace.

Call to Worship

Where is the one who is wise?
Where is the one who has understanding?
> **God alone is the source of true wisdom.**
> **Let us draw near to God!**
The wisdom from above is first pure, then peaceable.
It is gentle and willing to yield, merciful and fruitful.
> **In God there is no trace of hypocrisy.**
> **Let us draw near to God!**
A harvest of righteousness is sown in peace
for those who make peace.
> **If we draw near to God, God will draw near to us.**
> **Let us all draw near to God!**

OPENING PRAYER

God of wisdom, you welcome children of all ages into your loving arms and your gracious care. We gather in hopes of a better world, placing all our trust in you to make it a reality. Come to us!

CALL TO CONFESSION

If we have envy and selfish ambition in our hearts, we must not boast or be false to the truth. These things only breed chaos and disorder in our lives. If we are dissatisfied with what we have been given, then we have either failed to ask for the right gifts, or we have asked wrongly. Therefore, let us submit ourselves to God, not with pride, but with humility, remembering that we are but children.

PRAYER OF CONFESSION

O God, who has called us not to be great by human standards, but to be great in service and humility, we confess that we have been corrupted by values other than your own. We take for granted the freedoms of adulthood, but forget the obligations of maturity and forsake the joys of childhood. Purify our hearts and minds, and renew your living Spirit within us so that, by our good and godly living, we might show that our works are done with gentleness, born of wisdom, in the name of Jesus.

DECLARATION OF FORGIVENESS

Insofar as we resist evil and rebuke those who tempt us to wrong, evil will flee. And if we draw near to God, God also draws near to us, cleansing and protecting us from all evil and lifting us out of our humiliation. As you have confessed your sin to Christ, now leave that sin for Christ to banish, and walk away from it. You are free, and freely forgiven in Christ. There is no going back.

PRESENTATION OF TITHES AND OFFERINGS

The wise one is industrious with money and provisions, providing for family, reaching out to the needy, and treating the poor openhandedly. Those who fear the LORD are to be praised, and they will share the fruit of their labors. With wisdom, strength, dignity, and kindness, let us share what we have from God.

Prayer of Dedication

God of Grace, we seek to be servants, entrusting these offerings to your care. May they be used to teach our children all about you, to guide them in the righteous way, and to raise them in your holy name. May all your children, young and old, learn by Jesus' example of self-giving, and may we glorify you by extending to the poor and lonely, the humble and the heartbroken, both charitable alms and open arms in the Spirit of Christ's love.

The Blessing

Walk in the righteous way, and God will watch over you.
Welcome others with the loving arms of Jesus,
and you will find Christ in your embrace.
Show by your good works you are possessed of the Spirit of wisdom,
and your neighbors will be richer for knowing you!

Proper 21

Ordinary Time 26 / September 25–October 1

Esther 7:1–6, 9–10; 9:20–22

Psalm 124

James 5:13–20

Mark 9:38–50

IN PREPARATION FOR WORSHIP

You who are our help and stay,
who rescue us from the enemy,
who free us from the fowler's snare,
who spare us from the whelming flood—
you who sent your Son to save us,
we trust you with our lives.

CALL TO WORSHIP

Come, all who wish to act with mercy!
   All who give but a cup of water
   in the name of Christ will be rewarded!
Come, all who are sick! Come, all who are suffering!
Come, all who are in need of prayer!
   The prayer of faith will save the sick,
   and the LORD will raise them up!
Come, all who are cheerful and who long to be righteous!
   The prayers of the righteous are powerful and effective!
Come, all who wish to glorify God!
   Anyone who does a deed of power can only praise the LORD!
   Let us all sing songs in praise of God!

Opening Prayer

Watchful God, if you had not been on our side, we would have been lost long ago. But our help is in your holy name; in you, the Maker of heaven and earth! We bless you, O God, our Creator and Keeper, for in Christ you have snatched us from the countless snares of sin and the raging tide of evil.

Call to Confession

Whatever causes us to stumble along the journey of faith is to be thrown into the fire and burned. That we do stumble is undeniable. What then shall we burn? Let us not hide from God the sin in our lives. Rather, let us offer it up to be burned in the sanctifying fire of the Holy Spirit, and ask for Christ's purifying grace.

Prayer of Confession

Saving God, we confess that we have excluded others because we have not considered them a part of us. We are quick to find fault with people of difference and slow to admit the good that you do through them. Reform and renew our sinful hearts, and help us love you and all your people with greater humility.

Declaration of Forgiveness

Be at peace with one another. God has preserved and saved you. Live life now on your guard against sin, making prayer and obedience to Christ's rule of love your top priorities. Support one another. Keep each other from stumbling. Be healed of all that has weighed heavily on you, and do not return to your former ways.

Presentation of Tithes and Offerings

How better to remember God's kindness to us than by sharing our gifts with one another and with those in need. Let us celebrate God's goodness. Let us rejoice that the risen Christ has turned our despair into hope, our depression into joy, our mourning into the dawning of a new day. Let us offer our gifts in the Spirit of Christ.

PRAYER OF DEDICATION

For every reprieve you have granted,
for every blessing bestowed,
for every breath you have given,
for every debt now paid, once owed,
for every sign or glint of heaven,
for earthly love and suffering,
for every heart of sin repented:
O Blessed God, for every grace, we thank you,
and we offer you these signs of our love, in Jesus' name.

THE BLESSING

Find your help in the name of the LORD, who made heaven and earth.
Place your trust in the name of Christ, who died and rose for you.
Discover your power in the Holy Spirit, who meets you in prayer,
who stirs in you a desire to pray,
and may your life in the realm of God be renewed.

Proper 22
Ordinary Time 27 / October 2–8

Job 1:1; 2:1–10
Psalm 26
Hebrews 1:1–4; 2:5–12
Mark 10:2–16

IN PREPARATION FOR WORSHIP

Lord, I love this place in which you dwell,
and every place your glory abides.
Weigh and test my heart and mind,
that I might open to you and find
my hands washed, my sins erased,
my voice raised in grateful praise.

CALL TO WORSHIP

The steadfast love of the LORD is before us.
Let us walk in faithfulness to God.
> **We stand on solid ground when,**
> **in the great congregation, we bless the LORD.**
Vindicate those who trust in you, O God.
For we seek to live with integrity.
> **We stand on solid ground when,**
> **in the great congregation, we bless the LORD.**
Redeem and be gracious to us, O God,
so that we might tell of your wondrous deeds.
> **Our God is the ground on which we stand!**
> **With the great congregation, we bless the LORD!**

Opening Prayer

Holy Spirit, infuse our worship. The children of God are seeking Jesus. Holy Jesus, receive our worship. The children of God are seeking your kingdom. Holy God, attend our worship. Your family is gathered around your throne.

Call to Confession

Jesus Christ has tasted death for everyone and forged purity in place of our sins. Let us openly confess our sin to the Lord, entrusting God to forgive us, asking that our sins, as well as our selves, might be converted to God's good purpose.

Prayer of Confession

We cannot pretend we are guiltless, O God. We can only admit our sin, for everything is visible to you in the eternal light of your glory. Therefore, we ask to be made clean, washed but not swept away, by the Spirit, the water, and the blood of your suffering servant, Jesus Christ. Forgive and renew us, O God; make our hearts fit for truth.

Declaration of Forgiveness

God has made the pioneer of our faith, Jesus Christ, perfect through sufferings and, in doing so, brings God's children to glory. Christ, who has sanctified us, shares the same Father with us. For this reason, Jesus is not ashamed to call those whom he saves his brothers and sisters. Let us take our place before the throne of grace and give thanks to God that, in Jesus Christ, the firstborn of all creation, we are forgiven.

Presentation of Tithes and Offerings

Christ is the appointed inheritor of all things. Through Christ the world was created, along with everyone and everything in it. What do we own, what can we claim, that Christ has not already inherited? Let us offer to God that which belongs to the commonwealth of Christ.

Prayer of Dedication

We tithe not only when we feel inspired to do it, not only when things are going well. As God is the constant source of all our blessings, so we must also persist in our integrity, blessing even when it hurts, even when it seems we have no more to give. Let us bless the Lord, no matter what our situation. In plenty or in poverty, let us give good gifts to God.

THE BLESSING

Enjoy the holiness of life in the Spirit.
Walk with renewed integrity in Christ.
Receive the kingdom of God like a child,
and be a rich blessing to all whom you meet.

Proper 23
Ordinary Time 28 / October 9–15

Job 23:1–9, 16–17
Psalm 22:1–15
Hebrews 4:12–16
Mark 10:17–31

In Preparation for Worship

Compassionate Father, you know our weakness.
Suffering Spirit, you hear our lament.
Crucified Christ, you share your nature with us
through your death and our brokenness.
We struggle toward you, O God,
you who are the one and only answer
to the world's endless questions.

Call to Worship

Commit your cause to the LORD!
Let God be your deliverer.
> **You alone are holy, O God Most High!**
> **You are enthroned upon our praises!**
In God our ancestors trusted.
They trusted the LORD and they were saved.
> **You alone are holy, O God Most High!**
> **You are enthroned upon our praises!**
Do not be far from your people, O God!
For trouble is always near, and you alone are our help!

You alone are holy, O God Most High!
We are gathered for your glory!

OPENING PRAYER

Holy God, who calls us into eternal life, we cannot enter your kingdom without first acknowledging our accountability to you. Come and examine us with your wisdom, speak your penetrating word, bring it to life within every heart, so that the worship we offer to you in service might be worthy of your holy name.

CALL TO CONFESSION

The word of God is living and active, sharper than a two-edged sword. It is able to judge the thoughts and intentions of the heart. Before God, no creature can hide, but all are naked to the eyes of God, to whom we must answer for our living. Therefore, since our only real choice is the course of honest humility, let us express the burdens we carry, laying bare our hearts to God as we confess our sin.

PRAYER OF CONFESSION

O God, you who repay us, in this life, one hundred times what little we sacrifice, how slow we are to trust in you! We have forsaken certain gains for fear of risk; we have missed your joy for fear of suffering. Forgive us, O Lord, for all our sins, those of omission and commission, so that we might experience for ourselves and tell the world in new ways, that with you all things are possible.

DECLARATION OF FORGIVENESS

You who fear the LORD, praise him! All you children of the Most High, glorify him! For God does not despise the affliction of the afflicted. God has not hid his face from you but has heard and answered your cries of distress. Christ Jesus, our high priest, sympathizes with our weaknesses. Indeed, he himself has been tested in every respect, as we are; yet he who was found sinless has made good our account. Therefore, receive from his grace the mercy he offers you, and live for him!

PRESENTATION OF TITHES AND OFFERINGS

Never compare yourself to your neighbor, but compare your generosity with that of the Lord. Be humble, then, and imitate the free grace of God, who sets you free from bondage to earthly and temporal things.

PRAYER OF DEDICATION

Your grace, O God, makes us bold to approach you to offer these gifts to you. Your goodness, O Christ, makes us eager to tell the world of you, to proclaim your name to this and to future generations. Your holiness, O Spirit, makes us humble enough to recognize that our gifts are not ours alone, but you alone can render them effective to win the lost, to bless the poor, and to raise the dead. Gracious, good, and holy God, bless these gifts, that through them, and in all things, your will may be done.

THE BLESSING

Live to God who alone is good,
who loves you and has sent the Son to save you.
Live for Christ, the Son of God,
who has redeemed you from sin and who leads you to the Father.
Live in the fullness of the Holy Spirit,
who teaches you and reminds you, guides, directs, and protects you,
that you might enter fully into the kingdom of God.

Proper 24
Ordinary Time 29 / October 16–22

Job 38:1–7 (34–41)

Psalm 104:1–9, 24, 35c

Hebrews 5:1–10

Mark 10:35–45

IN PREPARATION FOR WORSHIP

O God of Majesty and Might,
who stands the waters above the mountains
and rebukes the waves so that they flee,
who rides the chariot of the clouds
and soars upon the wings of the wind:
Your wind and fire proclaim your word!
Your glory surrounds and protects us!
My soul will bless the LORD my God,
for you, O Mighty One, are very great!

CALL TO WORSHIP

Who has the wisdom to number the clouds,
or to summon the lightning?
Bless the LORD, O my soul!
For you, O God, are clothed with majesty!
Who has put wisdom in the inner being?
Bless the LORD, O my soul!
For you, O God, are wrapped in light!
Who determined the dimensions of the earth,
or laid the cornerstone for its foundation?

How manifold are your works, O God!
In wisdom you have made them all!

OPENING PRAYER

We welcome you, our Gracious Lord, into your holy sanctuary. We bow toward your holy throne. We ask you to tabernacle here, to hear our songs of thanks and praise, to receive our offerings of self and service, so that we might honor you by living solely for you.

CALL TO CONFESSION

Jesus, our perfect high priest, has humbly submitted to God in obedience and offered his life as a ransom for many. Christ is the source of eternal salvation for all who likewise obey and submit. Let us confess our need of this atoning gift.

PRAYER OF CONFESSION

Merciful God, with tears and cries you offered yourself for our release, yet our pettiness perpetuates grief and suffering. Forgive us, O Christ, for failing to recognize you in those we hurt or tear apart. Forgive us for holding ourselves and each other hostage in judgment, anger, contempt, and criticism. May your Spirit flow through us once again.

DECLARATION OF FORGIVENESS

God hears the prayers of Jesus, who rules in righteousness on our behalf. Our great high priest is begotten of God and does not seek self-glorification, but he willingly and lovingly serves all who would humbly accept the gift of God's perfect and total forgiveness. Be not proud or dismayed or disheartened. The Lord of all forgives you!

PRESENTATION OF TITHES AND OFFERINGS

To walk in the way of our Lord Jesus Christ, we must not expect to be served, but to serve one another in humility and love; we must not expect to receive, but to give of ourselves freely and selflessly. In joyful obedience to our self-giving Savior, let us reverently honor God with our gifts.

Prayer of Dedication

Creator God, the heavens proclaim your wonderful glory, the earth is
full of your wisdom. You have made your whole creation a blessing, and
revealed to us our place among the lowly. Therefore, we would defer to
your divine will, and render these gifts in humble gratitude for the grace
by which we are saved through Jesus Christ our Lord.

The Blessing

Go forth in the name of Jesus Christ,
make no pretension to superiority,
deal gently with those who go astray,
serve one another with meekness,
encourage one another with kindness,
and may the LORD Most High
smile at your humility.

Proper 25
Ordinary Time 30 / October 23–29

Job 42:1–6, 10–17
Psalm 34:1–8 (19–22)
Hebrews 7:23–28
Mark 10:46–52

IN PREPARATION FOR WORSHIP

O Jesus Christ, our perfect high priest,
you have offered yourself for our forgiveness and healing.
Thank you for your perfect offering,
and for the freedom we have in knowing
that you have made it,
once and for all.

CALL TO WORSHIP

Look to the LORD and be radiant,
so your faces shall never be ashamed.
> I sought the LORD, and God answered me,
> and delivered me from all my fears!
Walk to the LORD and be saved,
and your eyes will see all things new.
> I had heard of God with my ears,
> but now my eyes have seen the LORD!
Many are the afflictions of the righteous,
but the LORD rescues them from them all.
> O magnify the LORD with me,
> and let us exalt God's name together

OPENING PRAYER

O God, you provide for all who seek you, you redeem the lives of all who serve you! Though we are but dust and ashes, we will bless your holy name forever! Preserve us, O LORD, in this your holy sanctuary.

CALL TO CONFESSION

Jesus Christ's priesthood is forever! Our Lord is forever able to save anyone and everyone who approaches God through him. Christ lives to make intercession for all who approach God. Furthermore, Christ the Son and God the Father are in perfect agreement, holiness, and purity. Let us confess our sins through the one who is perfect and who has the capacity and the will to bring us to perfection.

PRAYER OF CONFESSION

Holy God, we confess that we have spoken of things we do not understand, things too wonderful for us, which we do not know. We have presumed too much and trusted you too little. Forgive us, O God. Restore our sight, rekindle our awe, and reform our speaking, so that the vision with which you bless us, and the shout that we send up, might be a celebration of your saving grace, even in the midst of a world that is lost and searching.

DECLARATION OF FORGIVENESS

Those who look to the LORD will never be put to shame! God has heard your cry and answers those who seek the LORD! Happy are all who take refuge in God, for none are condemned who take shelter in the LORD! Take heart! Have courage! Be of good cheer! Know that, in Christ, you are forgiven!

PRESENTATION OF TITHES AND OFFERINGS

Jesus Christ has made the perfect offering to God in giving himself on our behalf. What sort of offerings shall we then make? Not perfect ones, no, but honest expressions of thanks and praise with the very best we have to give.

Prayer of Dedication

May your praise be continually in our mouths, your love forever in our hearts, your word forever on our minds, your spirit forever urging us into acts of giving—and may each of these gifts, and each of these givers, find a holy purpose in the growth and glory of your kingdom.

The Blessing

May your eyes be opened to the glory of God around you;
may your ears be open to the call of Christ;
may you be responsive to the Spirit of Truth within you,
that the world might be healed by the trust you place in God!

Proper 26
Ordinary Time 31 / October 30–November 5

Ruth 1:1–18
Psalm 146
Hebrews 9:11–14
Mark 12:28–34

IN PREPARATION FOR WORSHIP

Holy God of Love,
may I draw nearer to you now than I ever have before;
may I love you with greater love than I ever have before;
may I know you with greater joy than I ever have before!
Holy God of Love, receive me,
though I am unworthy,
into your Holy Love.

CALL TO WORSHIP

Praise the LORD!
Let there be unity and agreement among the people!
>**Praise the LORD!**
>**Let us love God with all our hearts!**

Praise the LORD!
Let there be harmony in God's sanctuary!
>**Praise the LORD!**
>**Let us love God with all our minds!**

Indeed, you shall love the LORD with all your soul and with all your strength!
Let all who trust in God be filled with joy!

Let us love the LORD, who reigns forever!
Praise the LORD! Praise the LORD!

OPENING PRAYER

Faithful God, you are our God forever! Your love is constant; your ways
are fruitful. Wherever you lead us, we will seek to follow. Whatever you
ask us to do, we will seek to do with love. May nothing ever separate us
from you, O God. May we sing your praises with each day that we are
given.

CALL TO CONFESSION

Jesus Christ is, at the same time, both Lamb of God and God's High
Priest, who has entered the Holy Place, once and for all, and offered his
own blood to purify our consciences of dead works to worship the living
God. In confession, let us submit all our sins to the One who is able and
willing to take them all away.

PRAYER OF CONFESSION

O Christ Jesus our Lord, to you, the high priest of the good things to
come, we confess that we have let ourselves be bound by the past. Free
us for love, we pray! To you, the source of eternal redemption, we con-
fess that we have observed lesser laws than love. Redeem us for love,
we pray! To you, who entered the most holy place that is not of this
creation, we confess that we see with earthly eyes. Open our eyes to love,
we pray! We cannot trust ourselves, or any mortal, for our salvation!
Only you can help us. In you alone we hope and trust!

DECLARATION OF FORGIVENESS

Happy are those whose help is the God of Jacob, whose hope is in the
LORD their God! For the LORD sets the prisoners free, the LORD opens the
eyes of the blind, the LORD lifts up those who are bowed down. Rejoice
in the LORD, all you people! Be of one mind. For Christ our Lord has
offered himself through the eternal Spirit, and obtained for us eternal
redemption!

Presentation of Tithes and Offerings

The people of God know very well that the LORD is able not only to bring life, but to bring eternal life, out of grievous, broken, and barren situations. Therefore, bind yourselves to the God who redeems, pledge yourselves to the community of faith, and dedicate your whole heart and a goodly portion of your gifts to the works of the LORD and the Spirit of Love.

Prayer of Dedication

Holy and Eternal Spirit, in whom our Lord Jesus Christ has made the perfect offering of eternal love, we thank you for all that you have done and for all that you are doing on our behalf and on behalf of this troubled world. As our hands lift up these gifts to you, let our minds and hearts so join in the Spirit of Christ's perfect outpouring, that we may glorify you as he does, in unity, in harmony, in joy, and in love.

The Blessing

You are free to love the Spirit of God, for Christ our Lord has set you free. You are free to love your neighbor as yourself, for the ties with which we are bound together are only as binding as the free love of God. Go in peace.

All Saints' Day
November 1 (or *First Sunday in November*)

Isaiah 25:6–9

Psalm 24

Revelation 21:1–6a

John 11:32–44

In Preparation for Worship

Make your home among us, LORD,
for we would see the glory of God!
You who are the first and final,
make with us your home eternal!

Call to Worship

Come to the mountain of the LORD your God!
For God has prepared a rich feast for all peoples!
Destroy, O LORD, the shroud that lies over us!
Remove the veil that covers all the nations!
Let the LORD wipe away the tears from your eyes!
Let the LORD remove shame from the earth!
Let your word renew heaven and earth!
Let your word unite your new heaven and new earth!
Be glad and rejoice in salvation from God!
This is the LORD for whom you have waited!
You are our long-awaited God, our Savior!
You have swallowed up death forever!

Opening Prayer

Compassionate God, you not only have the power over life and death, but in your deep love for us, you accompany us through every moment of grief and triumph. Speak, that we may hear you, and by our hearing let us come to life, let us come to deeper faith in you.

Call to Confession

Let the old things pass away: death and mourning and crying and pain. Surrender them all to the LORD your God, who is busy making all things new: the new heaven, the new earth, the new Jerusalem like a new bride. That bride is not only the heavenly communion of the saints; she is the soul of each one who trusts in the Christ to take away every disgrace, the glorified body of the believer who accepts salvation from God. Let us confess our need and desire for this gift and our faith in the One who gives it.

Prayer of Confession

Holy God, we confess that we are tightly bound by the ways of the world, by sin and the power of death. Our hands are not clean, our hearts are not pure, and we have lifted up our souls to what is false and does not satisfy. We are not worthy to ascend your holy hill or enter into your presence. Forgive us, Lord. Purify us. Unbind us from our grave clothes and summon us to new life, for we are helpless to save ourselves. Our hope is in you alone!

Declaration of Forgiveness

The words of the LORD are trustworthy and true. The first things have all passed away. Christ Jesus is the Alpha and the Omega, the first and the last, the beginning and the end. It is he who commands that the stone be rolled away. Receive your vindication from the God of your salvation. In Christ Jesus, Lord of the Resurrection, your sins are eternally forgiven. The LORD has spoken. It is done.

Presentation of Tithes and Offerings

The earth is the LORD's and all that is in it, the world, and those who live in it. So let our giving be an act of public proclamation that nothing in our lives belongs to us, but all things—indeed, we ourselves—belong to God.

PRAYER OF DEDICATION

We give you thanks, O God, for you have provided for our hearing of the gospel, the joyful news of the resurrection life, by the Word of Christ and through the ministry of your saints through the ages. Looking back, we remember with gratitude those servants who fostered our first steps toward you. Looking around us, we see those whom you have given us to share in faith the earthly struggles of this life. Looking forward, we know that we can do nothing better for the inbreaking of your heavenly kingdom than to offer you all that we have to give, for the upbuilding of the everlasting communion of the saints. This we do in Jesus' name!

THE BLESSING

Lift up your heads and look! For the Savior of the World is coming!
Christ the King of Glory is coming to raise us into eternal glory!
Lift up your heads and look! For the God of the Living,
with the saints and with all the power of the Holy Spirit,
is coming again to make all things new!

Proper 27
Ordinary Time 32 / November 6–12

Ruth 3:1–5; 4:13–17
Psalm 127
Hebrews 9:24–28
Mark 12:38–44

<small>IN PREPARATION FOR WORSHIP</small>

God of Peace and protector of the poor,
we forsake the stale bread of anxiety
and seek instead the bread of your Living Word.
We turn our hearts to you, the only one who is truly just,
so that our living and our dying,
our worship and our praying,
our singing and our suffering,
may not be in vain.

<small>CALL TO WORSHIP</small>

Unless the LORD builds the house,
those who build it labor in vain!
    O LORD, be the builder of this your temple!
Unless the LORD guards the city,
those who guard it keep watch in vain!
    O LORD, be the protector of these your people!
May our life and work not be in vain!
Therefore, let the LORD be the true God over all our living.
    May all our offerings, both great and small,
    be great in love, and compassion, and justice!

Opening Prayer

Holy God, as Christ appeared in your presence on our behalf, we ask that you would raise us up, as his body, the Church, into your heavenly courts. Receive us, though we are lowly, into your glory and into your joy, that your name might be magnified throughout all the earth.

Call to Confession

God restores us when our spirits run dry, and nourishes us even when we feel like withering. In Christ, God has taken away every reason to fear condemnation, for with Christ there is payment and mercy, forgiveness and grace. Therefore, set aside your fears and step forward in trust, surrendering all your sins to God.

Prayer of Confession

God of the humble, you see every offering and know every heart. We come to you confessing that we are too weak and frightened to offer you everything, yet we strive to do so, in faith. Break down our resistance to you and make us defenders of those whom the world breaks down in the name of greed and exploitation. We ask your mercy in Jesus' name.

Declaration of Forgiveness

Christ has entered into heaven itself, appearing in the presence of God on our behalf. Our high priest has offered himself, once and for all, to bear the burden of our sins. What is more, Christ is coming again to save those who eagerly await his return. Look with hope for the return of our Savior, even as you live in humility and gratitude for the gracious forbearance of God.

Presentation of Tithes and Offerings

Unless God is at work in our work, the work that we do will be in vain. Therefore, let us entrust our provisions to the Lord, whose guiding wisdom and gracious participation will bless this ministry in proportion to our faithfulness.

Prayer of Dedication

May our hearts and our actions be consistent, O Lord, in keeping with your perfect will for our life together, for our presence in this community, and for our testimony to this fallen world of the love of our Lord Jesus Christ. Give life and health and growth to the members of your body, and help us fulfill the mission that you would perform in us and through us.

The Blessing

The Creator God is at work in the humble.
Be humble, and God will do great things in you.
The Lord Jesus Christ is coming again!
Be hopeful, and Christ will not disappoint you.
The Holy Spirit is alive in you!
Be wakeful and watchful,
and the Spirit will make of you
a whole new creation!

Proper 28
Ordinary Time 33 / November 13–19

1 Samuel 1:4–20
1 Samuel 2:1–10
Hebrews 10:11–14 (15–18) 19–25
Mark 13:1–8

In Preparation for Worship

I seek your presence here, O God,
not so much by entering your temple,
but by inviting you to enter mine.
Neither does this body belong to your servant
but to your Holy indwelling Spirit.

Call to Worship

My heart exults in the Lord!
My strength comes from the Lord my God!
There is no Holy One like the Lord!
There is no Rock like our God!
The Lord is a God of knowledge!
By the Lord our God our actions are weighed.
The barren and empty shall be made full!
But the arrogant shall be forlorn!
The Lord kills and brings to life!
God raises the poor from the dust and ashes!
Guard the feet of your faithful ones!
But let the wicked be cut off in darkness!

Opening Prayer

We exult in you, O Lord Most High, for you have set the world on its pillars. You who thunder in the heavens, you will judge the ends of the earth. We cannot prevail by ourselves, O God. So hear our prayers. Grant our petitions. Look with favor upon your servants, for you are good to those who love you, and your anointed shall be exalted!

Call to Confession

Do not let yourselves be led astray by the lies of the lawless and the delusions of the deceitful. Do not let yourselves be alarmed by the wars and rumors of the fearful. Rather, let us have confidence to enter the sanctuary by the blood of Jesus, holding fast to the confession of our hope in Christ, whose single perfect offering takes away our sin.

Prayer of Confession

Holy God of justice and mercy, we confess our souls are deeply troubled by the state of the world around us, and the state of the world within us. We long for the day when all enemies of your righteousness will be as a footstool for your feet. Yet, we admit our own loveless words and lawless deeds. We have failed to keep fellowship with and encourage one another. We acknowledge that our hope has often wavered and we have frequently gone astray. Holy God of justice and mercy, give birth to our Savior Jesus Christ within us that the world around us might become your kingdom of love and light!

Declaration of Forgiveness

Receive the good news with the full assurance of faith. Keep the commandments of God in your mind. Allow the new covenant to be written in your heart. Let your conscience be cleansed by Christ's total sacrifice. It is the Lord's perfect work that ensures your salvation; you need not depend on your own! Hallelujah!

Presentation of Tithes and Offerings

Can you even begin to count the number of times the Lord has granted your petitions, answered your prayers, kept you from trouble or rescued you, and given you all that you have needed besides, even those things for which you had not known or thought to ask? By the LORD alone will we prevail. By Christ alone are we made strong. Let us offer our gifts in exaltation of the LORD our God.

PRAYER OF DEDICATION

We exalt you, O LORD our God, for your generosity is abundant. We bow to you, O Jesus Christ, for your offering on our behalf is holy, all sufficient. We return to you, O Spirit of Life, in grateful response for your benediction, a portion of your gifts to us, for your wise use and loving distribution. Provoke us and move us to provoke one another to good deeds, to loving words in your most holy name, for we long for and we see your Day is fast approaching.

THE BLESSING

Jesus has opened a new and loving way for us to live eternally.
So may the Creator Spirit bless the children of God
in the body of Christ forever!

Proper 29
Ordinary Time 34 / November 20–26
(*Christ the King* or *Reign of Christ*)

2 Samuel 23:1–7

Psalm 132:1–12 (13–18)

Revelation 1:4b–8

John 18:33–37

IN PREPARATION FOR WORSHIP

O Alpha and Omega, who was and is and is to come,
you have made us to be your holy realm, priests in service to our Creator.
Free us from all earthly sins, take us up to your heavenly courts,
join our hearts with the seven spirits, ever in worship before your throne!

CALL TO WORSHIP

The LORD has chosen Zion.
God has desired it for a holy habitation, saying,
> "This city shall be my resting place forever;
> here I will reside, for I have desired it."
The LORD has blessed the people with abundance.
God satisfies the poor with bread:
> "I will clothe my priests with salvation,
> and my faithful will shout for joy!"
The LORD has sworn to his servant David;
God has promised and the promise is fulfilled:
> "One of your sons I will set upon your throne.
> If your children keep my covenant and my decrees,

their children also shall sit upon your throne."
Children of God, let us worship Christ our King!
To Christ be all glory and honor forever! Amen!

OPENING PRAYER

Lord Jesus Christ, your realm is not of this false world, but you reign in truth! We seek a place in your holy kingdom, listening for your voice, praying for the courage to testify that you alone are Sovereign over all Creation!

CALL TO CONFESSION

Those who have no fear of God are like thorns that are thrown away. They will not allow themselves to be touched by love or handled even with care. But those who fear God will also trust God to do what is best for them. Like patients with a doctor, they will tell God where it hurts, and so allow the healing process to begin. In reverence for our God and with a teachable spirit, let us honestly offer our sinfulness for God to examine, confessing our need for the tender mercies of Jesus Christ.

PRAYER OF CONFESSION

Sovereign God, we admit that we have allowed ourselves to be ruled by principalities and powers, idols and influences that bear no resemblance to you. We have participated in the violence—economic and ecological, social and domestic—of the nations of this world, all to our own supposed advantage. Lord, have mercy upon us. Allow us to come under and remain in your rule of grace and truth and love, so that the damage we have done might be undone, and that you may reign over our lives in peace.

DECLARATION OF FORGIVENESS

All glory be to Jesus Christ, who loves us and has freed us from our sins at the cost of his very own blood, who redeems the fruitless lives of sinners and with them establishes a holy kingdom, a priestly people, in service to God. Therefore, be clothed in the new garments of God's righteousness, and let all God's faithful shout for joy! Claim the forgiveness that is yours in Jesus Christ!

Presentation of Tithes and Offerings

God has blessed us with abundant provisions. Where God's Word and Spirit are present, even the poor are satisfied with bread. Now is the time for us to act on the Word and to be moved by the Spirit. Let us share what we have in common, as companions in truth, under the eternal reign of Christ.

Prayer of Dedication

Giver of all gifts, you know the great measure by which you have blessed us. In you, our diverse needs and assets are shared, and we find ourselves equally dependent on your mercy and kindness. With deep gratitude we offer these gifts to your glory, in Jesus' name, for the realm where the Spirit of truth is at home.

The Blessing

Christ is Sovereign over all Creation:
Therefore, be subject to God's creative reign.
Christ is the Word, alive and enthroned:
Therefore, be obedient to Jesus' rule of life.
Christ is the Truth, spoken forever:
Therefore, be attuned to the Spirit of Truth.
And may the reign of God be manifest
in all that you do.

Index of Scripture Readings

TEXT	EVENT	PAGE
Genesis 1:1–5	First Sunday After Epiphany—Ordinary Time 1	33
Genesis 9:8–17	First Sunday in Lent	66
Genesis 17:1–7, 15–16	Second Sunday in Lent	69
Exodus 12:1–4 (5–10) 11–14	Maundy Thursday [ABC]	96
Exodus 20:1–17	Third Sunday in Lent	72
Numbers 21:4–9	Fourth Sunday in Lent	75
Deuteronomy 18:15–20	Fourth Sunday After Epiphany—Ordinary Time 4	42
Ruth 1:1–18	Proper 26—Ordinary Time 31	204
Ruth 3:1–5; 4:13–17	Proper 27—Ordinary Time 32	210
1 Samuel 1:4–20	Proper 28—Ordinary Time 33	213
1 Samuel 2:1–10	Proper 28—Ordinary Time 33	213
1 Samuel 3:1–10 (11–20)	Second Sunday After Epiphany—Ordinary Time 2	36
1 Samuel 3:1–10 (11–20)	Proper 4—Ordinary Time 9	138

TEXT	EVENT	PAGE
1 Samuel 8:4–11 (12–15) 16–20 (11:14–15)	Proper 5—Ordinary Time 10	141
1 Samuel 15:34—16:13	Proper 6—Ordinary Time 11	144
1 Samuel 17: (1a, 4–11, 19–23) 32–49	Proper 7—Ordinary Time 12	147
1 Samuel 17:57—18:5, 10–16	Proper 7—Ordinary Time 12	147
2 Samuel 1:1, 17–27	Proper 8—Ordinary Time 13	150
2 Samuel 5:1–5, 9–10	Proper 9—Ordinary Time 14	153
2 Samuel 6:1–5, 12b–19	Proper 10—Ordinary Time 15	156
2 Samuel 7:1–11, 16	Fourth Sunday of Advent	12
2 Samuel 7:1–14a	Proper 11—Ordinary Time 16	159
2 Samuel 11:1–15	Proper 12—Ordinary Time 17	162
2 Samuel 11:26–12:13a	Proper 13—Ordinary Time 18	165
2 Samuel 18:5–9, 15, 31–33	Proper 14—Ordinary Time 19	168
2 Samuel 23:1–7	Proper 29—Ordinary Time 34 *(Christ the King or Reign of Christ)*	216
1 Kings 2:10–12; 3:3–14	Proper 15—Ordinary Time 20	171
1 Kings 8: (1, 6, 10–11) 22–30, 41–43	Proper 16—Ordinary Time 21	174
2 Kings 2:1–12	Last Sunday After Epiphany *(Transfiguration Sunday)*	57
2 Kings 5:1–14	Sixth Sunday After Epiphany / Proper 1—Ordinary Time 6	48
Esther 7:1–6, 9–10; 9:20–22	Proper 21—Ordinary Time 26	189
Job 1:1; 2:1–10	Proper 22—Ordinary Time 27	192
Job 23:1–9, 16–17	Proper 23—Ordinary Time 28	195

TEXT	EVENT	PAGE
Job 38:1–7 (34–41)	Proper 24—Ordinary Time 29	198
Job 42:1–6, 10–17	Proper 25—Ordinary Time 30	201
Psalm 1	Proper 20—Ordinary Time 25	186
Psalm 1	Seventh Sunday of Easter	126
Psalm 4	Third Sunday of Easter	111
Psalm 9:9–20	Proper 7—Ordinary Time 12	147
Psalm 14	Proper 12—Ordinary Time 17	162
Psalm 19	Proper 19—Ordinary Time 24	183
Psalm 19	Third Sunday in Lent	72
Psalm 20	Proper 6—Ordinary Time 11	144
Psalm 22	Good Friday [ABC]	99
Psalm 22:1–15	Proper 23—Ordinary Time 28	195
Psalm 22:23–31	Second Sunday in Lent	69
Psalm 22:25–31	Fifth Sunday of Easter	117
Psalm 23	Fourth Sunday of Easter	114
Psalm 24	All Saint's Day / November 1	207
Psalm 24	Proper 10—Ordinary Time 15	156
Psalm 25:1–10	First Sunday in Lent	66
Psalm 26	Proper 22—Ordinary Time 27	192
Psalm 29	First Sunday After Epiphany—Ordinary Time 1	33
Psalm 30	Sixth Sunday After Epiphany / Proper 1—Ordinary Time 6	48
Psalm 29	Trinity Sunday	135
Psalm 31:9–16	Sixth Sunday in Lent *(Passion Sunday)*	84
Psalm 34:1–8 (19–22)	Proper 25—Ordinary Time 30	201
Psalm 36:5–11	Monday of Holy Week [ABC]	87
Psalm 41	Seventh Sunday After Epiphany / Proper 2—Ordinary Time 7	51
Psalm 45:1–2, 6–9	Proper 17—Ordinary Time 22	177
Psalm 47	Ascension of the Lord [ABC]	123
Psalm 48	Proper 9—Ordinary Time 14	153

TEXT	EVENT	PAGE
Psalm 50:1–6	Last Sunday After Epiphany *(Transfiguration Sunday)*	57
Psalm 51:1–12	Fifth Sunday in Lent	78
Psalm 51:1–12	Proper 13—Ordinary Time 18	165
Psalm 51:1–17	Ash Wednesday [ABC]	63
Psalm 62:5–12	Third Sunday After Epiphany—Ordinary Time 3	39
Psalm 70	Wednesday of Holy Week [ABC]	93
Psalm 71:1–14	Tuesday of Holy Week [ABC]	90
Psalm 72:1–7, 10–14	Epiphany [ABC]	30
Psalm 80:1–7, 17–19	First Sunday of Advent	3
Psalm 84	Proper 16—Ordinary Time 21	174
Psalm 85:1–2, 8–13	Second Sunday of Advent	6
Psalm 89:1–4, 19–26	Fourth Sunday of Advent	12
Psalm 89:20–37	Proper 11—Ordinary Time 16	159
Psalm 93	Ascension of the Lord [ABC]	123
Psalm 96	Christmas, First Proper [ABC] *(Christmas Eve)*	15
Psalm 97	Christmas, Second Proper [ABC] *(Christmas Morning)*	18
Psalm 98	Christmas, Third Proper [ABC] *(Christmas Day)*	21
Psalm 98	Sixth Sunday of Easter	120
Psalm 103:1–13, 22	Eighth Sunday After Epiphany / Proper 3—Ordinary Time 8	54
Psalm 104:1–9, 24, 35c	Proper 24—Ordinary Time 29	198
Psalm 104:24–34, 35b	Pentecost	129
Psalm 107:1–3, 17–22	Fourth Sunday in Lent	75
Psalm 111	Fourth Sunday After Epiphany—Ordinary Time 4	42
Psalm 111	Proper 15—Ordinary Time 20	171
Psalm 114	Easter Evening [ABC]	105
Psalm 116:1–2, 12–19	Maundy Thursday [ABC]	96
Psalm 118:1–2, 19–29	Sixth Sunday in Lent *(Palm Sunday)*	81
Psalm 118:1–2, 14–24	Easter *(The Resurrection of the Lord)*	102

TEXT	EVENT	PAGE
Psalm 119:9–16	Fifth Sunday in Lent	78
Psalm 124	Proper 21—Ordinary Time 26	189
Psalm 125	Proper 18—Ordinary Time 23	180
Psalm 126	Third Sunday of Advent	9
Psalm 127	Proper 27—Ordinary Time 32	210
Psalm 130	Proper 8—Ordinary Time 13	150
Psalm 130	Proper 14—Ordinary Time 19	168
Psalm 132:1–12 (13–18)	Proper 29—Ordinary Time 34 (Christ the King or Reign of Christ)	216
Psalm 133	Second Sunday of Easter	108
Psalm 133	Proper 7—Ordinary Time 12	147
Psalm 138	Proper 5—Ordinary Time 10	141
Psalm 139:1–6, 13–18	Proper 4—Ordinary Time 9	138
Psalm 139:1–6, 13–18	Second Sunday After Epiphany— Ordinary Time 2	36
Psalm 146	Proper 26—Ordinary Time 31	204
Psalm 147:1–11, 20c	Fifth Sunday After Epiphany—Ordinary Time 5	45
Psalm 147:12–20	Second Sunday After Christmas [ABC]	27
Psalm 148	First Sunday After Christmas	24
Proverbs 1:20–33	Proper 19—Ordinary Time 24	183
Proverbs 22:1–2, 8–9, 22–23	Proper 18—Ordinary Time 23	180
Proverbs 31:10–31	Proper 20—Ordinary Time 25	186
Song of Solomon 2:8–13	Proper 17—Ordinary Time 22	177
Isaiah 6:1–8	Trinity Sunday	135
Isaiah 9:2–7	Christmas, First Proper [ABC] (Christmas Eve)	15
Isaiah 25:6–9	All Saint's Day / November 1	207
Isaiah 25:6–9	Easter (The Resurrection of the Lord)	102
Isaiah 25:6–9	Easter Evening [ABC]	105
Isaiah 40:1–11	Second Sunday of Advent	6

TEXT	EVENT	PAGE
Isaiah 40:21–31	Fifth Sunday After Epiphany—Ordinary Time 5	45
Isaiah 42:1–9	Monday of Holy Week [ABC]	87
Isaiah 43:18–25	Seventh Sunday After Epiphany / Proper 2—Ordinary Time 7	51
Isaiah 49:1–7	Tuesday of Holy Week [ABC]	90
Isaiah 50:4–9a	Sixth Sunday in Lent *(Palm Sunday)*	81
Isaiah 50:4–9a	Sixth Sunday in Lent *(Passion Sunday)*	84
Isaiah 50:4–9a	Wednesday of Holy Week [ABC]	93
Isaiah 52:7–10	Christmas, Third Proper [ABC] *(Christmas Day)*	21
Isaiah 52:12—53:12	Good Friday [ABC]	99
Isaiah 58:1–12	Ash Wednesday [ABC]	63
Isaiah 60:1–6	Epiphany [ABC]	30
Isaiah 61:1–4, 8–11	Third Sunday of Advent	9
Isaiah 61:10–62:3	First Sunday After Christmas	24
Isaiah 62:6–12	Christmas, Second Proper [ABC] *(Christmas Morning)*	18
Isaiah 64:1–9	First Sunday of Advent	3
Jeremiah 31:7–14	Second Sunday After Christmas [ABC]	27
Jeremiah 31:31–34	Fifth Sunday in Lent	78
Ezekiel 37:1–14	Pentecost	129
Hosea 2:14–20	Eighth Sunday After Epiphany / Proper 3—Ordinary Time 8	54
Joel 2:1–2, 12–17	Ash Wednesday [ABC]	63
Jonah 3:1–5, 10	Third Sunday After Epiphany—Ordinary Time 3	39
Matthew 2:1–12	Epiphany [ABC]	30
Matthew 6:1–6, 16–21	Ash Wednesday [ABC]	63

TEXT	EVENT	PAGE
Mark 1:1–8	Second Sunday of Advent	6
Mark 1:4–11	First Sunday After Epiphany—Ordinary Time 1	33
Mark 1:9–15	First Sunday in Lent	66
Mark 1:14–20	Third Sunday After Epiphany—Ordinary Time 3	39
Mark 1:21–28	Fourth Sunday After Epiphany—Ordinary Time 4	42
Mark 1:29–39	Fifth Sunday After Epiphany—Ordinary Time 5	45
Mark 1:40–45	Sixth Sunday After Epiphany / Proper 1—Ordinary Time 6	48
Mark 2:1–12	Seventh Sunday After Epiphany / Proper 2—Ordinary Time 7	51
Mark 2:13–22	Eighth Sunday After Epiphany / Proper 3—Ordinary Time 8	54
Mark 2:23—3:6	Proper 4—Ordinary Time 9	138
Mark 3:20–35	Proper 5—Ordinary Time 10	141
Mark 4:26–34	Proper 6—Ordinary Time 11	144
Mark 4:35–41	Proper 7—Ordinary Time 12	147
Mark 5:21–43	Proper 8—Ordinary Time 13	150
Mark 6:1–13	Proper 9—Ordinary Time 14	153
Mark 6:14–29	Proper 10—Ordinary Time 15	156
Mark 6:30–34, 53–56	Proper 11—Ordinary Time 16	159
Mark 7:1–8, 14–15, 21–23	Proper 17—Ordinary Time 22	177
Mark 7:24–37	Proper 18—Ordinary Time 23	180
Mark 8:27–38	Proper 19—Ordinary Time 24	183
Mark 8:31–38	Second Sunday in Lent	69
Mark 9:2–9	Last Sunday After Epiphany *(Transfiguration Sunday)*	57
Mark 9:30–37	Proper 20—Ordinary Time 25	186
Mark 9:38–50	Proper 21—Ordinary Time 26	189
Mark 10:2–16	Proper 22—Ordinary Time 27	192
Mark 10:17–31	Proper 23—Ordinary Time 28	195
Mark 10:35–45	Proper 24—Ordinary Time 29	198

TEXT	EVENT	PAGE
Mark 10:46–52	Proper 25—Ordinary Time 30	201
Mark 11:1–11	Sixth Sunday in Lent *(Palm Sunday)*	81
Mark 12:28–34	Proper 26—Ordinary Time 31	204
Mark 12:38–44	Proper 27—Ordinary Time 32	210
Mark 13:1–8	Proper 28—Ordinary Time 33	213
Mark 13:24–37	First Sunday of Advent	3
Mark 14:1—15:47	Sixth Sunday in Lent *(Passion Sunday)*	84
Mark 15:1–39 (40–47)	Sixth Sunday in Lent *(Passion Sunday)*	84
Mark 16:1–8	Easter *(The Resurrection of the Lord)*	102
Luke 1:26–38	Fourth Sunday of Advent	12
Luke 1:47–55	Third Sunday of Advent	9
Luke 1:47–55	Fourth Sunday of Advent	12
Luke 2:1–14 (15–20)	Christmas, First Proper [ABC] *(Christmas Eve)*	15
Luke 2: (1–7) 8–20	Christmas, Second Proper [ABC] *(Christmas Morning)*	18
Luke 2:22–40	First Sunday After Christmas	24
Luke 24:13–49	Easter Evening [ABC]	105
Luke 24:36b–48	Third Sunday of Easter	111
Luke 24:44–53	Ascension of the Lord [ABC]	123
John 1:1–14	Christmas, Third Proper [ABC] *(Christmas Day)*	21
John 1:6–8, 19–28	Third Sunday of Advent	9
John 1: (1–9) 10–18	Second Sunday After Christmas [ABC]	27
John 1:43–51	Second Sunday After Epiphany—Ordinary Time 2	36
John 2:13–22	Third Sunday in Lent	72
John 3:1–17	Trinity Sunday	135
John 3:14–21	Fourth Sunday in Lent	75
John 6:1–21	Proper 12—Ordinary Time 17	162
John 6:24–35	Proper 13—Ordinary Time 18	165
John 6:35, 41–51	Proper 14—Ordinary Time 19	168

TEXT	EVENT	PAGE
John 6:51–58	Proper 15—Ordinary Time 20	171
John 6:56–69	Proper 16—Ordinary Time 21	174
John 10:11–18	Fourth Sunday of Easter	114
John 11:32–44	All Saint's Day / November 1	207
John 12:1–11	Monday of Holy Week [ABC]	87
John 12:12–16	Sixth Sunday in Lent *(Palm Sunday)*	81
John 12:20–33	Fifth Sunday in Lent	78
John 12:20–36	Tuesday of Holy Week [ABC]	90
John 13:1–17, 31b–35	Maundy Thursday [ABC]	96
John 13:21–32	Wednesday of Holy Week [ABC]	93
John 15:1–8	Fifth Sunday of Easter	117
John 15:9–17	Sixth Sunday of Easter	120
John 15:26–27; 16:4b-15	Pentecost	129
John 17:6–19	Seventh Sunday of Easter	126
John 18:1–19:42	Good Friday [ABC]	99
John 18:33–37	Proper 29—Ordinary Time 34 *(Christ the King or Reign of Christ)*	216
John 20:1–18	Easter *(The Resurrection of the Lord)*	102
John 20:19–31	Second Sunday of Easter	108
Acts 1:1–11	Ascension of the Lord [ABC]	123
Acts 1:15–17, 21–26	Seventh Sunday of Easter	126
Acts 2:1–21	Pentecost	129
Acts 3:12–19	Third Sunday of Easter	111
Acts 4:5–12	Fourth Sunday of Easter	114
Acts 4:32–35	Second Sunday of Easter	108
Acts 8:26–40	Fifth Sunday of Easter	117
Acts 10:34–43	Easter *(The Resurrection of the Lord)*	102
Acts 10:44–48	Sixth Sunday of Easter	120
Acts 19:1–7	First Sunday After Epiphany—Ordinary Time 1	33
Romans 4:13–25	Second Sunday in Lent	69

TEXT	EVENT	PAGE
Romans 8:12–17	Trinity Sunday	135
Romans 8:22–27	Pentecost	129
Romans 16:25–27	Fourth Sunday of Advent	12
1 Corinthians 1:3–9	First Sunday of Advent	3
1 Corinthians 1:18–25	Third Sunday in Lent	72
1 Corinthians 1:18–31	Tuesday of Holy Week [ABC]	90
1 Corinthians 5:6b–8	Easter Evening [ABC]	105
1 Corinthians 6:12–20	Second Sunday After Epiphany—Ordinary Time 2	36
1 Corinthians 7:29–31	Third Sunday After Epiphany—Ordinary Time 3	39
1 Corinthians 8:1–13	Fourth Sunday After Epiphany—Ordinary Time 4	42
1 Corinthians 9:16–23	Fifth Sunday After Epiphany—Ordinary Time 5	45
1 Corinthians 9:24–27	Sixth Sunday After Epiphany / Proper 1—Ordinary Time 6	48
1 Corinthians 11:23–26	Maundy Thursday [ABC]	96
1 Corinthians 15:1–11	Easter *(The Resurrection of the Lord)*	102
2 Corinthians 1:18–22	Seventh Sunday After Epiphany / Proper 2—Ordinary Time 7	51
2 Corinthians 3:1–6	Eighth Sunday After Epiphany / Proper 3—Ordinary Time 8	54
2 Corinthians 4:3–6	Last Sunday After Epiphany *(Transfiguration Sunday)*	57
2 Corinthians 4:5–12	Proper 4—Ordinary Time 9	138
2 Corinthians 4:13–5:1	Proper 5—Ordinary Time 10	141
2 Corinthians 5:6–10 (11–13) 14–17	Proper 6—Ordinary Time 11	144
2 Corinthians 5:20b—6:10	Ash Wednesday [ABC]	63
2 Corinthians 6:1–13	Proper 7—Ordinary Time 12	147
2 Corinthians 8:7–15	Proper 8—Ordinary Time 13	150
2 Corinthians 12:2–10	Proper 9—Ordinary Time 14	153

TEXT	EVENT	PAGE
Galatians 4:4–7	First Sunday After Christmas	24
Ephesians 1:3–14	Second Sunday After Christmas [ABC]	27
Ephesians 1:3–14	Proper 10—Ordinary Time 15	156
Ephesians 1:15–23	Ascension of the Lord [ABC]	123
Ephesians 2:1–10	Fourth Sunday in Lent	75
Ephesians 2:11–22	Proper 11—Ordinary Time 16	159
Ephesians 3:1–12	Epiphany [ABC]	30
Ephesians 3:14–21	Proper 12—Ordinary Time 17	162
Ephesians 4:1–16	Proper 13—Ordinary Time 18	165
Ephesians 4:25–5:2	Proper 14—Ordinary Time 19	168
Ephesians 5:15–20	Proper 15—Ordinary Time 20	171
Ephesians 6:10–20	Proper 16—Ordinary Time 21	174
Philippians 2:5–11	Sixth Sunday in Lent *(Palm Sunday)*	81
Philippians 2:5–11	Sixth Sunday in Lent *(Passion Sunday)*	84
1 Thessalonians 5:16–24	Third Sunday of Advent	9
Titus 2:11–14	Christmas, First Proper [ABC] *(Christmas Eve)*	15
Titus 3:4–7	Christmas, Second Proper [ABC] *(Christmas Morning)*	18
Hebrews 1:1–4 (5–12)	Christmas, Third Proper [ABC] *(Christmas Day)*	21
Hebrews 1:1–4; 2:5–12	Proper 22—Ordinary Time 27	192
Hebrews 4:12–16	Proper 23—Ordinary Time 28	195
Hebrews 4:14–16; 5:7–9	Good Friday [ABC]	99
Hebrews 5:1–10	Proper 24—Ordinary Time 29	198
Hebrews 5:5–10	Fifth Sunday in Lent	78
Hebrews 7:23–28	Proper 25—Ordinary Time 30	201
Hebrews 9:11–14	Proper 26—Ordinary Time 31	204

TEXT	EVENT	PAGE
Hebrews 9:11–15	Monday of Holy Week [ABC]	87
Hebrews 9:24–28	Proper 27—Ordinary Time 32	210
Hebrews 10:11–14 (15–18) 19–25	Proper 28—Ordinary Time 33	213
Hebrews 10:16–25	Good Friday [ABC]	99
Hebrews 12:1–3	Wednesday of Holy Week [ABC]	93
James 1:17–27	Proper 17—Ordinary Time 22	177
James 2:1–10 (11–13) 14–17	Proper 18—Ordinary Time 23	180
James 3:1–12	Proper 19—Ordinary Time 24	183
James 3:13–4:3, 7–8a	Proper 20—Ordinary Time 25	186
James 5:13–20	Proper 21—Ordinary Time 26	189
1 Peter 3:18–22	First Sunday in Lent	66
2 Peter 3:8–15a	Second Sunday of Advent	6
1 John 1:1—2:2	Second Sunday of Easter	108
1 John 3:1–7	Third Sunday of Easter	111
1 John 3:16–24	Fourth Sunday of Easter	114
1 John 4:7–21	Fifth Sunday of Easter	117
1 John 5:1–6	Sixth Sunday of Easter	120
1 John 5:9–13	Seventh Sunday of Easter	126
Revelation 1:4b–8	Proper 29—Ordinary Time 34 (*Christ the King* or *Reign of Christ*)	216
Revelation 21:1–6a	All Saint's Day / November 1	207